D1461910

The Goldberg Variations

The Goldberg Variations

MARK GLANVILLE

Flamingo

An Imprint of HarperCollins*Publishers*

Flamingo
An Imprint of HarperCollins*Publishers*
77–85 Fulham Palace Road, Hammersmith, London w6 8jb

Flamingo is a registered trademark of
HarperCollins*Publishers* Limited

www.**fire**and**water**.com

Published by Flamingo 2003
1 3 5 7 9 8 6 4 2

Copyright © Mark Glanville 2003

Mark Glanville asserts the moral right to
be identified as the author of this work

A catalogue record for this book
is available from the British Library

ISBN 0 00 711841 4

Typeset in Perpetua by
Palimpsest Book Production Limited,
Polmont, Stirlingshire

Printed and bound in Great Britain by
Clays Ltd, St Ives plc

For Joshua and Arabella

Were the wind to blow even slightly against them
My eyes would refuse to close
HITTAAN BIN AL-MU'ALLAA

ACKNOWLEDGEMENTS

This is a work of non-fiction. Certain names and locations have been changed to protect identities.

I owe a huge debt of thanks to a number of people who eased the gestation of this book. David Miller, with his acute perception, intelligence and kindness, was all I could have wished for in an agent. At Flamingo the patient guidance and expertise of Philip Gwyn Jones have been inspirational, while Georgina Laycock's laser-like mind has helped bring the final sculpture into sharper relief. I would also like to thank Mark Lucas, without whose prompting I would never have written this book, Frederic Raphael, David and Mary-Lou Crown, and, above all, Julia, for the help and guidance they have given me. Lastly I want to thank Mum and Dad whom I love as friends as much as parents. I hope they'll forgive my frankness.

CONTENTS

I must own that I could have assured any questioner that Combray did include other scenes and did exist at other hours than these. But since the facts which I should then have recalled would have been prompted by voluntary memory, the memory of the intellect, and since the pictures which that kind of memory shows us preserve nothing of the past itself, I should never have had any wish to ponder over this residue of Combray.

Swann's Way, Marcel Proust

ARIA

What makes me myself rather than anyone else is the
very fact that I am poised between two countries, two
or three languages and several cultural traditions. It is
precisely this that defines my identity.

Les Identites Meurtrieres, Amin Maalouf

Happy the man who can celebrate his diversity. I wonder how
long, if at all, it took the author of the above to reconcile
the disparate elements of his own personality, to recognise
that they could live in harmony, and that his identity was
a compound of them. For a large part of my own life the
contradictory elements of my identity have been at war, and
have fragmented rather than fused me. Despairing of any
reconciliation, I've often wished or plotted for the destruction
of all but one of them (which depended on my changing mood),
so that I and it might live in peace thereafter. What follows is
an account of that campaign.

'So Abey goes into a mensvear shop . . .'

Sometimes we'd go into ourselves, his captive audience
perpetually on hand to applaud a nightly stand-up that ran
until we'd all left home.

'I vont to buy a suit!'

With a shift of the jaw his face would fall comfortably into
a parody of a ghetto Jew's cheek-straining smile.

'I think I can help you, sir,' the shop assistant would reply with the bright, clipped elocution of the forties public-school-boy Dad had been.

There were certain jokes that bore umpteen retellings. Mum was usually the first to laugh, with a hearty whoop to convince you she'd never heard it before, then we'd come in, each a different note on the xylophone counterpointing the melody of his speech.

'Here we are. If you don't mind . . . slipping it on . . . that's right . . .'

By now he'd be treading the amtico tiles that formed his stage, miming the appropriate movements of his dramatis personae.

'But look! It's coming up here,' he'd cry as the Jew, hunching his right shoulder in a gesture ludicrous enough to silence the percussion of our dining.

'Er, do excuse me, sir, but if you don't mind my saying, that's because you're not standing properly. Now if you were to . . . that's it. Splendid!'

'But now it's coming out here!'

The sight of Dad's head between his shoulders, jacket hunched, a Jewish tortoise, snapped our last resistance and earned him the laughter he yearned for. At such times we were a team, playing catch with smiles round the table, listening for each other's laughter with an unspoken sense of belonging engendered by the joke and its teller.

'Sir, you're still not standing properly. Now if you . . . That's it . . . Excellent!'

'Vunderful! A perfect fit!'

Bending his doppelgänger double, he'd exit his imaginary shop as a Yiddisher Quasimodo.

'So he's walking down the street like this, when he bumps into his old friend Morrie.

'"Keneine hora! Abey, vot happened to you?"'

We didn't know what the Yiddish meant, but it was a meal in itself. You could bite into the boiled chicken and smell the pickled cucumber.

'"I've just been to see my tailor."'

By now he'd be really milking it, Abey growing ever more grotesque as Dad hobbled up and down the kitchen.

'"To see your tailor. I should go to see your tailor. Vot a vunderful tailor he must be! Vy, if he can fit a cripple like you he can fit anyvun!"'

And as Abey, Morrie, the tailor and the narrator left the stage, five suns formed a spotlight he could bask in, Dad's 'Thank you, thank you,' reflecting our joy back at us with a nod and a bow.

Family life was played out around a circular kitchen table. The court of King Brian and his fair queen Pamela was a boisterous one at which each bite of food gained was a soundbite lost. We'd peck away incessantly at meat and conversation, all fighting to be heard and fed, picking up the debris left behind in the wake of Dad's voracious appetite and machine-gun verbal barrage. He had a favourite image of someone eating as if Cossacks were about to swoop down and steal all his food; and speaking as if they were going to cut out the tongue that ate it, he might have added. We children developed habits of our own to survive, one of which was speed-eating. Liz, twin to Toby, extended this to speech, cramming extraordinary quantities of words into the millisecond gaps that occurred when Dad caught his breath or swallowed a chicken thigh, while I'd try speaking louder in the hope of engaging at least one other person in conversation, but woe betide any dialogue that threatened to drown the monologue.

'Keep it down to a dull roar could you! Heard a good one the other day. Why do they have dustbins at Polish weddings? To keep the flies off the bride.'

'Your Dad's being very naughty.'

'Fucking Poles!'

'Brian!'

'Sorry, mutteler, those damned Poles,' he'd correct himself in pre-war officer tones before returning to those of the public school that he always joked had cost his parents a fortune.

'Worse than the Germans. They couldn't wait to get at us.'

'Brian, can we stop this?'

'Three million killed in Poland alone,' he'd sigh, energy draining from his face. 'And they let so many of them over here along with those bloody Ukros.'

It was ironic that, wracked daily with the torments of the Holocaust, we should be living two doors away from the Ukrainian Cultural Institute of Great Britain, which was founded and frequented by men who were reputed to be former members of the Waffen SS.

'Brian, you're so filled with hatred. You have to learn to forgive. At least you didn't lose anyone. Never a week goes by when I don't think of poor Theo. One has to carry on. I don't under*stand* why you're like this.'

He'd cast me an ally's wink. This was a scene that played at least once a month.

Jokes blessed us. They bottled an essence of something that belonged to children denied the ordinary trappings of identity portrayed on the labels of religion and suits. After all, we didn't even own our name. Around 1880 my Lithuanian great-grandfather, a quack dentist, arrived in Ireland. By the turn of the century his sons were all qualified and practising in Dublin. After moving to London and marrying an East End Jewish girl, my grandfather opened a telephone directory at random and out popped the Anglo-Norman house of Glanville whose scions would doubtless have had little time for him and his kind as they passed through the Rhineland en route for Jerusalem. Thus poor Goldberg, having survived a thousand years of persecution, assumed the name of one of his tormentors. After Dad was sent to Charterhouse, where he could acquire the mannerisms to complement the new name, the deception became complete.

Mum hadn't heard such jokes before she met Dad. Her father had been brought up in Prussian Breslau, now Polish Wroclaw, one of those middle-European cities of uncertain identity where Jews flourished, in which people weaned on wienerschnitzel and sauerkraut would have winced at the odour of lokshen soup, even if they might have eaten the carrot on the head of the gefilte fish. Deluded German Jews, Yekkes, revelling in the fruits of an emancipation not enjoyed by their kindred to the east, began calling their children Siegfried, after the hero of Wagner's myth of Teutonic superiority, oblivious to the fact that it was his enemy Alberich, the ugly, covetous dwarf whom the composer envisaged as the prototype Jew. Meanwhile in their synagogues the plangent wail of the cantor was drowned beneath the organ-accompanied congregational wash flowing in from the church across the road.

There was nothing obviously Jewish about Mum. Her delicate,

Reform nose captured the more refined scents that wafted past Dad's Orthodox schnoz, and she laughed in hearty major keys. Another Morrie, who worked in another menswear shop, this one up the road from us in Notting Hill Gate, once described her to a colleague as 'the tall woman with the jovial manner', and it was a description Dad never let her forget. It was how she often seemed, but though she laughed in jolly, perfect intervals, it was really in response to the vibrations of a plaintive instrument, one she and Dad both owned, and which we, their children, had inherited. It was hard to imagine her as anything other than English, and impossible to believe that she, who always sounded so aristocratic, should have arrived in England barely able to speak the language. Despite her tolerant, forgiving approach to the Holocaust in which members of her family had been murdered, and the little attention she paid her Jewishness, it was she rather than Dad who never felt comfortable or at home in England. Dad's Jewishness was far more belligerent, but, born and bred here, he'd assimilated, while Mum was a true foreigner, as German as she was Jewish. Like so many Yekkes she maintained a pride in German culture that overrode the ghastliness the country of its origin had visited on her people. My own feelings of alienation had more in common with Mum's sense of non-belonging than with Dad's soapbox stances.

After the fashion of 'better' Germans, Mum's father had been sent to be educated in England. There he met his gentile wife, 'the Ethiopian in the fuel supply' as Dad called her, quoting WC Fields; according to Orthodox Jewish laws of matrilineal descent, she, our only non-Jewish grandparent, was the only one whose status mattered when it came to determining which side of the gentile/Jewish divide we fell. After waiting for him while he was interned on the Isle of Man during the First World War as an enemy alien, my grandmother followed him to Holland, the place of his repatriation, giving birth to my mother in Amsterdam whence they returned to Berlin. They remained there until 1933 when he was granted a visa allowing him to emigrate to England, his reward for the indignity of having to train up a young Nazi journalist on the *Berliner Tageblatt*. By the time she was twelve, Mum had already worn more suits than Dad would have to wear in his entire life.

While we washed up and dried the dishes, Dad would sing. Like an old-time music-hall performer, he could do a bit of everything.

'Brian, are you just going to sit there all evening singing songs, or can we have some help?'

'*Sit here, just here all evening singing songs . . .*'

There wasn't a word, a phrase, a situation that didn't remind him of some ghastly old number he'd immediately begin to croon.

'Oh Brian, shut up!'

'*Shut up, that's how I am without you. Shut up, alone and blue . . .*'

Pavlov's dog had learned many commands, but his howl was melodious.

'Where on earth do you get all those dreadful old songs?'

'I'm a philistine, mutteler, but a lovable one.'

In the contrast between Mum's polite, old-fashioned soprano and Dad's earthy baritone, one heard the difference between the environments that had nurtured them. Snatches of lieder, the German songs Mum had heard as a girl, came to her intermittently, like her reminiscences of 1920s Berlin. Dad's world was as clear as a photograph, but Mum's was more like a jigsaw whose pieces she sometimes threw us but which we were never able to complete. There were parts of it we weren't allowed to see, so the lieder became important, capturing something of the essence of Mum's background, as songs and jokes did Dad's. It was practically the only time we heard her use German, a language she claimed, somewhat strangely, she no longer spoke. Mum's rendition of Schubert's 'Heidenroslein' was my first acquaintance with a composer whose music was always able to take over for me at the point where words could no longer describe feelings. Schubert's setting matches Goethe's simple moral tale of a boy who sees, plucks, and is pricked by a beautiful rose, with an even simpler accompaniment, but the painful thorns which so often accompany beauty, wound a vocal line the cheerful accompaniment can never quite heal. It captured the essence of my mother.

For her the kitchen in the basement was less a domain than a prison where three meals had to be prepared each day and served on a table at which the places were always neatly laid – once the washing-up was finished it was usually time to start cooking again. She was never quite alone down there, even when we'd all gone to bed and Dad was off at a football match or upstairs watching *Kojak*. Something was incarcerated with her that would sometimes vent its frustration by hurling things around and occasionally make an unwelcome appearance; a small child she sometimes mistook for one of us, that only she had ever seen. In time Mum's poltergeist became Dad's scapegoat when no one else could be blamed for the not infrequent disappearance of his personal possessions, as if he subconsciously perceived it as the agent of her ill will.

'There's no other explanation. It's been polted,' he'd complain, though it struck me that the confusion of competing files, bags and newspapers in his study, where items as large as footballs could remain hidden for weeks, was a far more likely explanation. The poltergeist's unhappy presence somehow reflected her own predicament, tied below stairs. It frightened a couple of au-pairs; one ran up the stairs screaming after a mirror was lifted off its hook and thrown to the floor with a crash. But though we were told it drew on our childish energy, we only saw the effects of its actions once, when a loaf of bread mysteriously rose from the work surface and hovered in mid-air before falling to the floor. Even Dad was upstaged that evening.

I was envious of Mum's relationship with the poltergeist. It meant she was capable of inhabiting worlds denied the rest of us. I knew Mum had special gifts. She understood the healing qualities of music, when our imaginations had been over-stimulated by tales of entities such as the poltergeist in the basement. Once or twice it appeared in the hall, though that was as far as it went. Something was tying it down, preventing release into the realms she and it would have preferred to inhabit. I guess it came to remind her of that fact, as much as to sympathise with her sense of captivity. Confronted with such a reflection of her own dilemma, no wonder she felt afraid.

VARIATION ONE

The Football Hooligan

VARIATION ONE — *The Football Hooligan*

There's no need to be afraid in the hall. You just have
to pretend to be the ghost who might meet you there
(from The Ego and its Mechanisms of Defence by Anna Freud)

'The main trouble is that he has never really accepted the
arrival of the twin brother and sister, who were born when
he was two years old. Their birth threw him into turmoil
which manifested itself in many obvious and wretched
ways. He became and has remained heavily dependent
on and involved with me. There is a predilection for
sadomasochistic situations and the beginnings of a pleasure
in the idea of whipping. Also he shows a potential for
pervert tendencies such as a compulsion to look at and
to feel girls' pants. While he tends to be bullying and
aggressive at home he is on the whole placatory and
nervous at school, and not very popular. In his actual
work he is doing well, showing a special interest in
History and English.'
Pamela Glanville to Dr Winnicott, letter, 1967.

Early history is the bastard child of personal recollection and
other people's anecdotes. Its objects, like the ghosts and
monsters that flit in and out of view in old penny arcade
machines, are glimpsed fleetingly. Some, including my own
family, employ psychotherapists to bust these machines and
compel their images to stay in view long enough to be assessed

and analysed. I was sent off to track mine down at eight, when Mum wrote her letter to Dr Winnicott, but I can't say I came away with a more focused picture of childhood than those who never had the benefits of therapy. To me childhood is still a lost play of which scant tangible evidence remains; fragments quoted by others, discovered on papyrus, inscribed on stone.

An early talkie is probably the oldest piece in my archive. Stripey-uniformed nanny Jeanette buckles my harness abruptly with jolts and bumps and hauls me behind her as she pushes a pram containing my new twin brother and sister towards Kensington Gardens.

'You're not walking properly!'

Whack! Her hand comes down across the side of my face like a whip: it stings. My cheek goes warm, almost comfortingly so. I still can't keep up.

'You're not walking properly!'

Whack! This one catches me across the side of my head and makes me think about what I'm doing with my feet. Although I try to correct them, I find myself stumbling and tripping. Again and again her hand comes down. Much fainter is the reel of her shoving me against a stone step and smashing my tooth. The incident where she hurled me across the kitchen with such force that I hit the wall, landing half-conscious on the floor is someone else's first-hand testimony. The cleaning lady witnessed it, but she didn't want to cause any bother so she didn't tell Mum. When I told Mum about the regular beatings, nanny Jeanette denied it vehemently and she believed her.

Five years later Mum felt compelled to write a letter that

should have led to me being watched by Special Branch for the rest of my useful life.

. . . a compulsion to look at and to feel girls' pants — another ghost I can freeze-frame. The moment the girls lined up to have their arithmetic books marked was always the highlight of an otherwise dull day. When they were all in position I'd crawl forward on my hands and knees, looking up their skirts for the statutory grey knickers. Or else, I'd deliberately misbehave and have myself thrown out of Scripture, partly because I wasn't very good at drawing sheaths of corn, but chiefly because I knew the older girls would be doing gym then. I'd roam the corridors of the school, until I reached the hall through whose windows I could enjoy visions of pretty girls vaulting over horses and running about in their underwear.

After five, the images linger long enough for me to examine them without the crutch of hearsay. We had a succession of au pairs: Sylvia, Maria, Gerda, Brigitte, Ulrike. I remember Mum crying in the kitchen and holding her in the familiar squidgy embrace, feeling her tears roll down my cheeks and the shock of emotional reversal.

'Your father's always been the same, I was even warned about him, dancing off with other girls at parties.'

She'd tell me of the time she caught him 'smooching with some silly girl', and how she put on a Highland fling, grabbed a man at random and reeled past, bumping into him as hard as she could. She laughed at the memory and I guessed he'd seen the funny side too.

'Always the same type. He won't change. Once a woman-iser . . .'

A word that acquired heroic status in my mind. Other

boys could be engine-drivers or firemen, I wanted to be a womaniser.

I worshipped Dad. He was always around, as he worked at home. Page upon page emerged like the product of a twenty-six legged centipede dipped in ink. So long as I was quiet he'd allow me to sit with him, overlooked by a John Bratby painting in chunky, thumb-nail deep oil that years of indoor football eventually chipped away. Around the time I was able to translate its abstract shapes into men playing billiards, there's enough primary evidence and eyewitness testimony for my history proper to begin.

Now that I'm six I'm as clever as clever
And I wish I could be six now for ever and ever

sang Christopher Robin, and I believed him. All year I'd been reciting those lines as a mantra that promised to see off the ills of infancy. I'd crossed the first threshold and I could see rewards beyond it. Good things happened in autumn. Boots and hats and coats and gloves and scarves smothered me against the *foggy foggy dew* Dad often sang of. The trees painted their multi-coloured pictures and every footstep was an adventure in which you might crackle, crunch or slide. Each week Mum and I walked to the Kensington children's library. Our jaunts recalled the golden days when I had no sisters, no brother Toby, a time before I was wrenched from Mum's lap and hurled into the world of the nanny beyond. Our twenty-minute walk was the magic of the annual journey to Santa's grotto repeated every week, and the books Mum and I chose, tales of witches, ghosts and other creatures living in fantastic realms, comforted me until the next visit. At night I kept my world alive even when the lights went out, continuing my reading with a torch under the sheets.

* * *

Dad started taking me to football matches. I'd sit with him in the press-box, for the first time allowed into a world that had been exclusively his. Not that I was entirely ignorant of it. I could name every team in the country, plus dinosaurs like Wanderers, Blackburn Olympic, and The Royal Engineers. I knew all the F.A. Cup winners, year-by-year, League champions, Charity Shield opponents, but my one love was Manchester United. I don't know why. It never occurred to me that they played a very long way from west London as I assumed that the entire universe bordered Holland Park Avenue and that if you went past North Kensington you'd fall off the edge. It didn't matter that my first game was Chelsea v Nottingham Forest. Even now I can visualise an all-blue Osgood streaking through helpless red shirts to score the only goal of the game. A comforting, enveloping mist came off the damp wooden seats, the playing turf, from the mouths of ranked journalists, and the mugs of tea served at half-time. In those days, the players were as magical as the immortals I read about by torchlight. In my second game I saw Rodney Marsh score a hat-trick in a 4–0 QPR victory over Watford. His name echoed round Loftus Road to the accompaniment of a massive bass drum. I then started watching Dad's own team, Chelsea Casuals, on the pitches in front of Wren's Royal Hospital alongside the Chelsea pensioners in their magnificent red and navy uniforms and wondered how long it would be before I'd be able to play for them myself.

Sport was always the bond between me, Dad, and eventually Toby. It was one that divided the family on gender lines. One day Dad appeared in the nursery with a long, green box.

'Okay, kid. Let's see what you're made of!'

His grin revealed a wolf's crowded jaw in all its splendour.

The pine table in the nursery where we normally ate our cornflakes was about to be transformed into a ping-pong table. Dad ripped apart the cardboard and hurriedly assembled the net with the eagerness of a lynch mob erecting a gallows. I juggled the ball on my bat. Having seen off all comers at a party recently, I was feeling pretty confident.

'Ready, kid?'

He served the ball gently and it bounced across the net, high enough for me to be able to smash it down on his side.

'Pretty good, kid!'

It was all going as I'd expected until I began to serve. The ball flew off the end of the table and under the battered red couch by the wall.

'The table's not long enough.'

'Excuses, kid.'

My game worsened with my growing frustration until, gradually, I mastered the short length of the breakfast table and Dad's gentle returns left plenty of room for winning shots.

'Okay, kid. How about a game? Play for service?'

Dad bounced the ball across the net and I returned it with ease, but my next shot spun off against the window.

'My serve.'

Dad chopped at the ball and it came across the net gently enough, but, as I attempted to return it, the ball spun off viciously and hit the window.

'1–0,' beamed Dad.

For some reason his serves were now impossible to return. 0–5 down, it was my turn to serve. I bounced the ball swiftly across the table where it clipped the end, veering beyond his reach.

'Blast!' cried Dad, his smile metamorphosing into a grimace. When my second serve achieved the same result, he flung the new bat down on the ground. I was concerned he'd break it. The next three serves were as fast and efficient as I could manage, but on each occasion my attempt to return resulted in the ball flying off in the opposite direction from the one I'd intended. As the score piled up against me, I simply couldn't understand why my shots were all miscuing. The tears welled behind my eyes as Dad's expression grew more and more triumphant.

* * *

I couldn't be six for ever and ever, so I was sent to The Hall, a pressure-cooker preparatory school in Hampstead where pink blazers emblazoned with black iron crosses made us targets for the kids from the local secondary modern.

. . . *he is on the whole placatory and nervous at school and not very popular.* My parents attacked this dilemma with a fork — psychotherapy on one prong, martial arts on the other. At the judo club in Vauxhall I came across kids like the ones from the secondary modern and got on fine. When they discovered I could stand on my head for five minutes at a time, everyone was summoned to watch my feat. Although they may have been smiling at a freak show, from my upside down vantage point even the glum faces were smiling. I could have stayed there for hours. I also learned Tai o Toshi, which I used to defeat the school bully. Heavy wooden desks and chairs flew in the hurricane of our combat.

> There's a motto shall ring in the ears of all
> Who e'er have spent their youth at The Hall.
> It's a call to the sluggard, the dull and the wise,
> A call we cannot and daren't despise.
> So now and for ever raise the call
> Hinc in altiora, up The Hall!
> There are overs and unders in life all through,
> In after life you'll get your due.
> If you keep up the struggle and never stop
> At the last Reading Over you'll come out top

I found this ancient piece of bombast beneath a pile of neglected sheet music. 'Overs' and 'unders' and 'Reading Overs' were still the yardstick by which academic success was judged forty years later. Everything we did was measured so we need be left in no doubt as to our level of achievement at any given time. Everything I enjoyed was tarnished by the incessant competition. In a school of three hundred there were 120 prizes and cups to be won. (I once sat down and counted them all just to make myself more miserable.) With such a ratio I should surely have won something. It was hard to believe Mum, Dad or any of my supporters and backers when all my best efforts failed to convince successive Hall judges and juries. Praise was mere flattery until quantified by competitive success, and Dad's anguish and irritation at each fresh defeat seemed sharper than my own. I felt I was failing him dreadfully. Conversely, on the one occasion when I did have some success, achieving an 'over' in every subject and gaining a gold star, my excitement was drowned in the torrent of his delight. I began to feel that achievement was his way of defining me. I'd listen to him discussing what I'd done, as if my actions were separate from their agent, and my existence could only be checked in terms of them. Being me simply wasn't good enough. But that was how he'd been brought up: each novel was a scalp for his mother's belt, worn at Bar Mitzvahs, weddings and funerals. Every Sunday, after the publication of a new novel, our stomachs experienced a collective tingling in anticipation of the reviews. He judged his work by them, and I knew that no matter how much he disparaged the scornful ones, they were the ones he believed.

Football was where I felt it most acutely. Dad never stopped assuring me of my ability, and while I could bounce the ball on my foot for twenty minutes at a stretch, swerve round defenders and strike goals, it was something I preferred to do in the playground, where there were no white lines and circles to circumscribe my enjoyment and no one lost their temper if you missed an open goal or shouted if you failed to save one. Playground football was fun, and one of the boys gave it colour with versions of chants he'd picked up from the Chelsea Shed.

Over there, over there.
In pink and black,
A load of crap

Not one you'd have heard tumbling readily from the lips of the Fulham Road barrow boys.

Dad's eyes were fixed on the school's Under-11 team. When

I did the trial, I was selected as substitute, which meant I had to run the line for a painful 70 minutes, chapping my thighs against the coarse, black woollen shorts.

'Did you get on. Did you get on?' he'd ask me every time I came home from a game, bounding down the stairs like an excited poodle.

It was the last game of the season. As I shivered in the downpour I imagined myself coming on, receiving the ball in midfield, flicking it out of the mud to swerve round the big bloke, building up pace and running between two defenders before rounding the goalkeeper to touch the ball into an empty net for the winning goal. By the time I got home fantasy had become reality; one that I knew would please Dad. I thought he was going to break into a triumphal dance. As he hugged me I wept into his bristly cheek, before running upstairs to my bedroom, hoping the pillow might suffocate me along with my shame.

* * *

Music gave me a language to cope beyond the thinking barrier. My only regret was when it had to stop with the angry utaca utaca of the stylus bumping over the edge of the vinyl onto the gap between harmony and the white noise on the label beyond. Besides listening I was also learning the clarinet. My teacher, Marjorie Dutton, was the only female staff member I had dealings with. Her gentle femininity contrasted starkly with the chalk-throwing, ear-clipping masters, but it was impossible to proceed down any path at The Hall for long before coming up against the obstacle of competition. I didn't want to go in for the Reisenstein Woodwind Prize, but I was persuaded that if I wanted to make progress I had to do so. On the night, instead of the usual mellow sound, a series of squeaks emerged, as from a fallen fledgling. I stopped and told the audience I would start again. In the gallery round the hall, the masters stood like statues above the shields of the great public schools whose scholarships and places the pupils marched confidently towards. Once again the fledgling sounded instead of Mozart. Again I stopped, and started again. At last the instrument began to sing. A sympathetic audience applauded loudly, acknowledging courage rather than virtuosity. Of course, I won nothing.

My gold star propelled me into the scholarship form. Suddenly I was in a class of strangers who didn't want to know me. They'd established their bonds, the strangest of which was with the form teacher himself, who used to confide the details of failed romances to his students. They took me aside and warned me that on no account should I discuss what I'd heard outside the class. Isolated, I soon slipped down the ranks, my gold star twinkling very faintly somewhere in the distance. The following term I was back among the common herd, labouring for a place at Westminster School. Prizes in singing and recitation whizzed past my nose. I started playing truant, with the collusion of my parents, at one stage staying off school for a full six weeks, and sat by Dad's side as he rattled off his first children's novel, *Goalkeepers are Different*. I tore each page from the typewriter in my eagerness to read the story, confirming to him that it had narrative drive and earning myself a dedication.

My parents began to research schools that specialised in music. The Purcell was out because it didn't have a football pitch. Pimlico, unfortunately, had several. A brand new comprehensive opened the year before I went there, it sought to attract what it called 'special musicians'. Unfortunately the course wasn't ready when I arrived in the summer, the only special musician in my year of three hundred. They compensated by releasing me from Woodwork and Religious Education to practise.

My late entrance to the class, special privileges and snobby accent in a school where everyone spoke Cockney, or pretended to, wearing the smart flannel blazer Mum had bought me rather than the standard woollen one, made me a prime candidate for bullying.

'What d'you wanna cam 'ere for? You should be at one of 'em posh places.'

Most of the boys seemed to want to fight me, and the girls to go out with me. Seemed being the operative word. Trysts arranged at the school gates were never kept. Academically the level was so far below the one I'd reached that I was simply treading water.

There was a fighting hierarchy at Pimlico; and Les and Ray were my bogeymen. Coming out of the science lab one afternoon, I was jostled and pushed as usual in the narrow corridor. A fist smacked my ear. It burned fiercely to the accompaniment of a painful, high-pitched whistle. The helplessness and humiliation hurt more.

'Ah look, Ray. You've made 'im cry.'

Up in the Geography class Les received his comeuppance for consistent minor offending. The teacher decked him with a couple of right handers that left him sprawled on the floor.

'You was laughin', Glanville.'

'' Course I wasn't.'

''E were, Les. 'E were laughin' atcher.'

'After the lesson, I'm gonna fuckin' do yer!'

Worse than the fights themselves was the anticipation. They were rarely spontaneous. More often than not a grudge would have to be avenged hours after the offence that had given rise to it. Much of my early time at Pimlico was spent in a state of panic as to what might befall me later.

Down on the dark concourse where no teacher trod, Les exacted his revenge. I tried to avoid the blows that bounced off my head, my cheeks and my back until an uppercut caught me in the nose with a crack. It didn't hurt much but the blood gushed over my white shirt and fell on the floor in little sticky piles as I scurried about like a frightened hen, trying to protect myself from further blows, wondering how much damage had been done.

'Go' 'im!'

'Nice one, Les.'

Job done, they walked away.

I did have a group of friends. They'd meet in the toilets and form a human arch against the wall, then each take it in turns to run a gauntlet of kicks and punches. Having experienced it once, I was assured that I couldn't leave the coven. Time and again they tried to force me back into these rituals with threats and beatings. One afternoon, waiting outside the Humanities class, two of them held me as a third laid into me with savage blows. My anger at this injustice and humiliation rose, but this time things were different. My arm cranked, and my fist flew round and into my tormentor's jaw with a satisfying smack.

As he reeled round, clutching his face, I relished the pain and astonishment in his eyes. The detention I received felt more like a reward than a punishment.

Practically everyone at Pimlico supported Chelsea: a circumstance that led me to become part of yet another minority there; though this time not of one. Chelsea had their attractions. One of the two best sides in the country at the time, they'd recently won their first F.A. Cup and their very name epitomised the stylish era we were leaving behind. Even the club song was played regularly on Top of the Pops, so it wasn't entirely inexcusable that I should choose Stamford Bridge to make my first foray onto the terraces, in the company of a sportswriter friend of Dad's. My parents had regaled me with horror stories about life down there among the yobs, away from the bourgeois comfort of the adjacent seated areas, so it came as a huge relief, not to mention a thrill, when I returned home unscathed after an uneventful match against Huddersfield Town.

Another opportunity to watch Chelsea from the terraces came my way when gorgeous Josie Lee asked me out on a date to see Peter Bonetti the Cat's testimonial against Standard Liege of Belgium. Needless to say, she followed her predecessors and failed to turn up, but this was a date I fully intended to keep with or without her. I wanted to be back on the terraces, this time not at some dull outpost as in the game against Huddersfield, but in the heart of the volcano. Approaching the Shed, I watched as the perpetual motion of the mass of close-packed bodies sent waves rippling to the extremities of the terraces beyond. At its heart I was surrounded by fag-smoking Artful Dodgers, kids who'd wipe the floor with the likes of Les and Ray, school rejects, yet kings of a domain my anonymity allowed me to be part of. 'The Liquidator' started up, skinhead reggae, its instrumental moonstomp rhythm met by synchronised handclaps and choruses of 'Chelsea'. Many wore the uniform of multi-eyed Doc Martens, two-tone trousers, Ben Sherman shirts, red braces and crew cuts. Lighted bangers flew through the air, exploding dangerously close to my face. As arms linked for 'Knees up Mother Brown' I was shoved hard in the back, fighting to keep my balance as row after dancing row cascaded down the steps, leaving vulnerable bodies prone in their wake as the waves returned to their source before starting all over again. I watched the coppers flying in, and hauling people out roughly, and relished the rawness, the danger in the faces and stances of people who spat, and spilled their steaming tea and chewed their burgers open-mouthed in a pungent haze of fried onions and beer-fuelled farts. There were no rival supporters, but even without them the atmosphere was charged with a sense of menace that left me shivering as I exited the ground, not with fear but elation. Feeling that I'd successfully completed a rite of passage, I experienced a warm tingle of acceptance, although sure no one there had even been aware of me.

* * *

My bent nose, like Cleopatra's, changed the course of history. Les and Ray were severely reprimanded and I was swiftly transferred to another class with only a week to go before the end of term.

We spent the summer holiday in Kent, where Toby and I played football on the village green situated conveniently opposite our family cottage. I'd wait at the window until there was a quorum, then sprint across the road to join them. If there were no football in the offing, I'd freewheel my bike down the steep hill round the corner, watching the speedometer hit thirty before joining the main road through the village. Our holidays there fell into a routine: Denton for cream tea, Canterbury for the cathedral, Hythe for the beach, and as Mum struggled to keep us all above the boredom threshold, Dad, an eternal Greta Garbo to be disturbed on pain of death or worse, would closet himself away to write his annual novel, emerging only to defend his honour at ping-pong or his goal on the village green. I became increasingly obsessed by the thrill of freewheeling, seeing how far I could push the pin on the dial, how long I could sustain the speed on level ground. One afternoon, pedalling like a maniac down the pavement, trying to keep at thirty, I thudded with a halt into the body of an old woman who had been emerging from the bus-shelter. High on panic I felt strangely detached from the situation of the prone, grey-haired figure on the ground and the miscued blows aimed at my head by her distraught husband. Out of the corner of my eye I saw the gold family estate car slowing down on the other side of the road and my brother, Toby, crying. The old man was too. I burst into tears and fled, convinced I was a murderer. In the distance I could hear an ambulance siren. Mum told me the old lady wore a pacemaker and might die.

I channelled my energies towards the garden, crucifying slugs, disembowelling woodlice, mixing red and black ant nests in the hope of seeing a war. When bored with insects, I'd sit on the wall at the front of the house and hurl crab-apples at the boys cycling past. One afternoon I hit my target several times and he swerved in front of a car. The screeching brakes, the smoke from the wheels and the pungent smell of burning rubber set doors opening and nets twitching. It was the second time I'd roused the village from its habitual sloth. Amiable, freckled John lay motionless in the road but the car, thank God, had managed to avoid him. Mum and Dad reckoned it had to be down to the new school. Disturbed adolescent, delinquent and neurotic, I was packaged and labelled, ready for delivery.

Autumn saw the arrival of the first official batch of elite 'special musicians', thirty or so, their rounded speech marginally reducing the playground twang quotient. The once quiet corridors of the music department now resembled an orchestra pit before the overture, a hubbub of competing strings and wind. With the door closed I could just about concentrate on polishing a Weber run, refining a Mozart adagio or perfecting the riff from *High Society*. I was obsessed with jazz, listened to it, played it, and read about it. One of the newcomers, a trumpet player called Philip, shared my enthusiasm. We'd go down Charing Cross Road and dig out New Orleans standards, then go home and work them out, singly and together. At home it was all we played, at school all we discussed when we weren't trying to recruit the trombone, piano, and bass we needed to form our own Red Hot Five. One morning Mr Spencer, the Head of Music, heard the first chords of the 'Jelly Roll Blues' strike up, sullying the nineteenth-century air that wafted past his rooms. His tie appeared at the window, the door opened and there he stood, skinny but towering, his eyes furious behind his spectacles. He glowered at the offending sheets as if they were hard-core pornography. I lived in Kensington, Philip in Stanmore, and the other prospective members of our combo, who could say? Banned from playing in school, the band had no future, so jazz became a solitary affair, a consolation if I was feeling down. Only it could help me clear the 'Can't play Jazz Blues'. I pictured my hero in *The Benny Goodman Story* sitting on the roof of his family's New York home and doodling to himself until the pretty girl arrives, as if conjured by his playing like a genie. No such genie answered my breaks although officially I had a girlfriend, one of the special musicians, a sweet violinist called Caroline with pillowfuls of red Irish hair. I'd lie on the bed with her, wondering what to do next, even though a classmate had taught me how to come, furnishing me with the crucial bit of information I was lacking.

'You gotta move it ap an' down!'

Clarinet in one hand and cock in the other, I had the restorative and the nostrum.

I integrated successfully into my new form with the aid of an image change. I'd outgrown the flannel blazer, and was able to persuade Mum that the commonly worn woollen variety would be warmer. I wore the fashionable attire of the terraces; pleated Ben Sherman or Brutus shirts, blue and green two-tone tonic trousers and tassel-loafer shoes. To top it all I had a navy blue, knee-length crombie, complete with red silk handkerchief tucked into the top pocket.

'Glanville thinks 'e's a skin'ead!' sneered one of the bitchier girls in the class, hitting the target with painful accuracy. Soon after a group of the genuine article surrounded me on the tube, swiped my handkerchief, and sat opposite, gloating over its quality and discussing how they'd pick the embroidered initials out of Mum's gift.

Every penny I had I spent on jazz, generally at HMV on Oxford Street, a twenty-minute bus ride away. One afternoon, with King Oliver's Dixieland Stompers and Jelly Roll Morton already in the bag, I headed for the cassette department. There it was, winking at me from the tidy rows, The Dutch Swing College Band, as if it knew I had no money left to buy it with. Mum, a huge jazz fan, had raved about them. I'd been trying to find one of their records for months. I glanced behind. Two shop assistants were chatting by the till. I looked left, right, in the mirror above. A short man in an old, brown mac stood next to me and began extracting and replacing cassettes aimlessly. Like me, I thought, up to no good. I felt very self-conscious and hot in the crombie as I turned the cassette round and round in my hand, peeling off the cellophane nervously before plunging it into the depths of my coat pocket. I walked through the store in a daze, my stomach tingling uncomfortably, until I was out in the dazzling autumn sunshine and someone gripped my shoulder. It was the man in the brown mac.

In the manager's office they kept me waiting half an hour while they debated whether or not to call the police. In the end I was released. As soon as I was home I rushed into Mum's arms and burst into tears, and, before you could say Carl Jung, I was flicking through *Country Life* in a Harley Street waiting room.

Sigmund Freud was one of the household gods. Handsome green volumes of his oeuvre lined the drawing-room bookcase, the works of the disciples by their sides. We were encouraged to read them almost as soon as we were out of nappies, not just the theory, but also its application in works such as *Moses and Monotheism* or *Civilisation and its Discontents*. My parents accepted his precepts unquestioningly. Theory was also put into practice. Mum was in therapy with a brilliant polymath in Reading, learning as much about zoology and Shakespeare as she did about herself. My brother and sisters all had counselling at one time or other. Only Dad didn't. He just sent everybody else off to be cured, hoping his life would be made easier once we had been. Had he been analysed himself we might all have benefited. Freud was good enough for us, but the barbs in his beard might spike Dad's muse.

My own analyst, Dr Woodhead, was a proper Freudian, old enough to have known the great man and grown up with the passion of a new faith. I'd lie on the couch while she sat behind me, white-haired and elegant in county tweeds, stopwatch ticking for fifty minutes, both happy with silence, and content to bounce questions back at me with a sure forehand. Our sessions were twice a week. I was ferried from school and then home by Douglas 'Buzz' Wells, an ex-racing driver, golfer and boxer with a toothbrush moustache who referred to her as Timbernut. The expensive navel-searching must have seemed indulgent to a man who'd resolved his own frustrations in the ring or on the racetrack. Our laddish conversations lifted the damp, analytical gloom my sessions left me wrapped in. A couple of visits a week to his place in Norland Square, just round the corner from my parents, might have benefited me more.

To the left and to the right of Sigmund Freud stood Groucho Marx and Lenny Bruce. Together they comprised a Jewish atheist's trinity. A diet of the sayings of these three topped up with a daily Holocaust catechism constituted our religious education. Hatred of our enemies defined my Jewishness as we weren't kosher, and didn't observe any of the holidays or festivals. In fact adherence to the central part of the Trinity deprived me of the sacred B'rith, the covenant of circumcision that binds all Jewish men to God. My Freudian parents thought it would lead to a castration complex. Dad certainly had one. He regularly informed me that Jewish women were domineering shrews to be avoided at all costs. He could get away with saying this as Mum was only half Jewish.

A central event in family lore was the Kossoff trial. The broadcaster, David Kossoff, had accused Dad of writing anti-Semitic handbooks, a slander that deeply upset both my parents. Mum's tears drove Dad to a court action which he won, conducting his own defence. It was a case that made the front page of the *Evening Standard*. Kossoff's main target, *The Bankrupts*, was in fact an unremittingly scathing and negative account of the idolatrous, philistine suburban Jewish world of ritual without religion that public school had allowed Dad to escape. 'Who likes the Yiden? The goyim hate the Yiden, the Yiden hate the Yiden. Nobody likes the Yiden,' my great-grandmother apparently used to say.

The only Jews I knew were Dad's friends from the literary and intellectual world like Frederic Raphael and Isaac Bashevis Singer, fascinating, charismatic people I could listen to for hours who would have shared his view of the environment he'd had to escape in order to define himself.

Jewishness seemed synonymous with non-religious values and aspirations (embodied by these people) which I cherished and admired. We saw little of Dad's family. His beloved father had died when I was a baby and his mother lived in Hove with her second husband Bobby, known to us as Uncle Booby, and there, as far as Dad was concerned, they could stay.

There had been plenty of Jewish kids at The Hall. At Pimlico I couldn't name one, which might explain why the words Jew and Hymie were bandied about so readily, demonising the absent race, substituting the Jew of anti-Semitic gentile folklore for the reality.

'Ere, Froggy! Gi's back that twenty pence wot I borrowed yer!'

'Ain't go' it, Dave?'

'Nah. Course you ain't, 'cos yer a fackin' Jew, incher?'

'Don't call him a Jew.'

Alan and Froggy stared at me, bemused.

'Why? 'O says 'e ain't?'

'If you want to say someone's mean, say so, but don't say they're a Jew.'

A smile stole across Alan's podgy, red face.

'Alright, Hymie!'

'Can we have silence over there, please?' yelled the teacher.

'Hymie, Hymie Goldberg.'

The silly, and basically harmless refrain spread across the row behind me, but I'd made them conscious of a usage that came too trippingly off their tongues. Now I'd got it out in the open there was more chance of being able to tackle it. It amused me they'd actually hit on my real name. I turned round.

34

'Just don't call someone a Jew if you want to say they're stingy.'

Again the refrain.

'Oy, Hymie!' Alan smiled. 'Comin' out to play football?'

As the pips went for the end of break and the drudgery of geography beckoned, I heard someone call out 'Nice goal, Hymie!'

It was Klewer. Twice the size of anyone else in the class, well liked for his friendly, open nature, but considered to be one of the best fighters in the school.

'Shame you 'ave to be so Jewish with the ball, though.'

I wanted to give him the benefit of the doubt, so I grinned but he didn't smile back.

'What's the matter, Hymie?'

The rage began to fill my chest. Before me stood the embodiment of the abuse and savagery inflicted on my people for two thousand years, that I heard recounted daily, that had led to Mum's cousin Theo being gassed at Auschwitz. I spat full in Klewer's face. I'd never seen him look angry before. He lurched towards me, a big brown bear.

'Fight! Fight!'

Other boys alerted the ones who hadn't made it back to the classrooms and I was aware of figures scurrying towards us. My only chance against this giant was to do a Muhammad Ali, so I moved in fast, through his cumbersome blows, and hung over his shoulder, not giving him the chance to swing, reducing his punches to pats and paws. If Klewer broke free I'd be in hospital.

'Come on, Klewer. Smack 'im!'

'Belt 'im!'

'Cam on, 'e's a wanker!'

I wondered how long I'd be able to hang on before the crowd's incitement mixed with his anger would cause the explosion to free him, but the blows began to peter out and eventually we separated. Klewer gave me a cold, unforgiving look.

'You're lucky!'

'Klewer could've killed yer!'

'Yeah! Knock sixteen colours o' shit aht o' yer!'

'Finish it later!'

My passion was spent. I looked at Klewer. He just seemed fed up.

I couldn't wait to tell Dad how I'd fought a bigger opponent in defence of my Jewishness.

'Filthy anti-Semitic bastard!'

'He's not. He's just ignorant.'

'Is he a Polack?'

'No idea.'

'With a name like Klewer?'

'Could be anything.'

I didn't need to forgive Klewer. I could have embraced the boy who'd allowed me to focus my sense of being Jewish so keenly.

Conversation at the court of King Brian flowed as normal that evening.

'You know what my friend the Irish watchmaker says, "Oi've always worked on the principal that every Goy is an anti-Semite, and d'you know what, Brian, Oi've never, never been proved wrong."'

'Oh, Brian,' Mum sighed. 'You're so filled with negativity.'

'Have you heard what happened to Mark today?' he answered, as if in explanation.

'Yes,' Mum sighed.

'It's always there, ready to rear its ugly head. I just thank God for the blacks and the Asians. They've taken the heat off us.'

'Visible targets,' I chimed in.

'That's right. As long as I don't show my profile,' Dad chuckled through his chicken. 'You know what your godfather says? "Er, nobody knows I'm Jewish, er, until they see me."'

We did, but we laughed anyway.

'At least you don't have that to contend with.'

'What do you mean?'

'Well, you don't look Jewish.'

'Of course I do.'

'Darling, you don't.' Mum's sweet tone heightened the provocation.

'You should be grateful for that,' Dad continued.

'For what? I'm not going to hide. They can all know I'm Jewish as far as I'm concerned.'

'But, my dear, you're not Jewish.'

'What do you mean? Of course I am.'

'By Jewish law you're not. Your grandmother was the Ethiopian in the fuel supply.'

Mum chortled.

'Seventy-five per cent of my blood is Jewish. It's what I am.'

'The wrong seventy-five per cent, schmendrick!'

'And why are you, who never goes near a synagogue, so

keen on upholding Jewish law? Only when it suits you, so you can have a go at me, undermine me, take the things I care about away from me.'

Dad simply sat there laughing, his poultry-filled belly heaving. It was always the same when he was cornered, his last defence. I pushed my chair over and kicked it aside, slamming the glass-panelled door behind me as hard as I could in hope it might break.

Upstairs I lay on my bed, watched from above by my own Holy Trinity of Best, Law and Charlton, centrepiece of a shrine dedicated to the saints and apostles of Manchester United. Silk and woollen football scarves pinned to the picture-rail framed the altar. Although this wasn't a great time to be supporting United, that only intensified the passion. To me being a United fan meant suffering, assuming the stigmata of the martyrs who'd died at Munich. I'd been too young to fully appreciate the glorious sixties that culminated in the European Cup triumph of 1968: my most cherished memory was of their winning the National Five-a-Side championship in 1970. Ever since dubious refereeing had disallowed a perfectly good Denis Law goal that would have sent us into the 1969 European Cup Final, the club had been in decline. Watching them on their trips to London was a joyless experience; regularly drubbed at Spurs and Arsenal, usually beaten by Chelsea and QPR, sometimes squeezing a draw at West Ham. Worst of all was the 5–0 thrashing at the hands of co-relegation strugglers Crystal Palace that left me weeping bitterly into my hand-knitted scarf. Ironically, we stayed up while they went down that year, but it felt as if it wouldn't be long before the bottom of the First Division opened and we were received into the maw of the Second.

At that time United fans were regarded as the most violent in the country. In reality they were no worse than many others, but there were so many of them. Ten thousand regularly travelled when the club played away, swamping rival supporters' ends. It was an environment considered too dangerous by my parents, so I'd watch them from the stands, part of me terrified by the red-and-white-clad northern hordes, a lot of me yearning to be in there with them.

* * *

Twenty minutes' walk from home we had one of the best sides in the country. The years since I watched Rodney Marsh score his hat-trick against Watford had seen QPR's fortunes wax as much as United's had waned. Stan Bowles was a worthy heir to Rodney, and the club had a plethora of fine players to carry on the good work of the late sixties. My parents thought (wrongly) that QPR's terraces met their safety standards. It wasn't the Shed, it wasn't the Stretford End, but I soon got to know the hundred or so regular faces that made up the Loft. I didn't really support them – love for United brooked no rival – but I was becoming hooked on the thrill of being accepted by clubs that wouldn't have me as a member, and on the adrenaline that flowed from fear and aggression.

'You'll never take the Lo-oft!' was one of the emptiest chants ever heard at a football ground. Chelsea, United, Arsenal and West Ham regularly did. Spurs were the most fun. There were so many of them we never had a chance, but we had a go anyway, holding the citadel just above the entrance while they repeatedly charged, trying to overwhelm the blue-helmeted line that separated us. Inevitably the dam would burst, sending wave upon wave of Doc-Martened skinheads pouring over us, boots and fists flailing indiscriminately. The big thing was not to go down. We'd retreat, leaving a sinister no-man's land while the coppers formed a new line and the Spurs fans filled the vacuum. Then we'd regroup and charge back at them, knowing it was futile, but the sheer exhilaration of racing across the terraces, not knowing quite what to expect, made it worthwhile. Eventually we'd merge into the crowd, little pockets of rebels for the Spurs fans to seek and destroy, and the game would continue to the accompaniment of the sporadic explosions that followed whenever they found us.

If the opposition were less well supported we might go hunting ourselves, though it normally ended in farce, as in the home Cup tie against Orient.

'The only way we're going to get the Labour Party back into power is by hanging onto our pipes,' announced one of our main faces, pipe between his teeth, in an imitation of Harold Wilson worthy of Mike Yarwood, but we were supposed to be looking for the opposition firm at the time. A small mob suddenly appeared on the other side of White City Way. They charged into us and a few seconds of the usual indiscriminate kicking and punching ensued until we realised it was Paul O'Reilly's firm and we were fighting our own side. Occasionally we'd run into individual fans who seemed up for it, but a code of fairness operated and it normally ended up one on one, even if our one tended to be the top boy.

* * *

Music was the catalyst for my first trip to Old Trafford. United v Spurs was my reward from Dad for gaining a distinction in my Grade Five clarinet exam. I practically had to run to match his pace as he headed for Holland Park station like an Olympic walker in training.

'Come on, panther!'

Just as I'd learned to eat and talk fast, so I'd been forced into an unnatural stride.

'But Dad, the train doesn't go for an hour and a half!'

I was speaking to my accompanying breeze.

By the time I turned into the station he was standing by the lift gate, green cardboard tickets in his hand, blue 1964 Olympics bag over his shoulder crammed with pink Italian sports papers and our packed lunch. As the lift operator pulled the heavy gates apart we heard the vacuum-cleaner sound of a train leaving the platform. And Dad was away, like a sprinter off his blocks.

'Dad! The train's gone!'

I was left, talking to a backpacker. There was no sign of Dad. As I reached the platform he was scurrying awkwardly towards the far end in anticipation of the change at Oxford Circus.

'Come on!'

He turned round anxiously as another train clattered into the station and I was forced to sprint the final yards. Shuffling along the edge of the platform as the train came to a halt, he secured a position by the opening doors and long-jumped on ahead of the opposition to reserve a couple of seats. A copy of *The Times* was thrust into my hands. It was several stops before I'd managed to restore it to its original, pre-breakfast form, and I'd barely established that Bobby Charlton was fit when we were at Oxford Circus, leaping like TV detectives through the opening doors into the crime scene.

As the escalator at Euston finally brought us back into the light I noticed groups of lads scattered about the concourse, most not wearing scarves, a few sporting tiny badges on which I could just about make out the United ship motif. Scars and earrings complemented the donkey jackets, bovver boots and drainpipe jeans they wore; one or two had United tattoos etched onto the sides of their heads and necks. Amidst them stood a group in dark grey jackets, and creased brown pin-stripes, looking, for all the world, like accountants, but as the mobs dispersed to a far-off platform, they fell into line with them.

'C-O-C-K-N-E-Y, Cockney Reds will never die!'

The war cry rang round the station.

'Like something to eat, dear?'

We'd scarcely sat down when out came lumps of food wrapped in silver foil, and a couple of cans of lager. Dad's wolf-like teeth tore at a chicken breast. He wrenched the metal ring from one of the cans with the sound of a piston firing, and a fine Heineken mist descended over my hair and face.

'Lovely grub!' he enthused.

The succulent pink flesh seemed to invite a ferocious response and, as I bit through the bone into the marrow, the shards splintered into the roof of my mouth. I was about to open my beer can politely in the direction of the window when I noticed a silver-haired man in suit and tie glaring at Dad, so, in filial solidarity, I turned it towards him and released it, to my disappointment, not with a whoosh but an unnoticed phip.

'Looking forward to it, dear?'

Such a tame phrase could never adequately describe my feelings. I was heading for the seat of my religion.

After Stoke the weather changed. Sheets of pine-needle rain frapped against the window.

'Here we go!'

Dad stuffed the silver foil and newspaper detritus back into his satchel and began heading up the train, bumping past scruffy, long-haired locals as the terminus came into view. I jumped off the moving locomotive onto a wet platform, the impetus carrying me into a sprint towards the ticket barrier. For once I was ahead of him.

As we made for the bus stop, rivulets of grime ran down the dilapidated brickwork of abandoned buildings. But to me, everything was transformed by association with United. Even the orange and white of the double-decker, so different from the plain red of the London variety, seemed as exotic as the singsong local accent that Dad seemed to hate so much. The bleak urban landscape and scattered housing estates glimpsed from motorway bridges looked like futuristic relatives of the Emerald City.

People began to leave their seats. I looked in vain for floodlights and wondered how long it would be before I saw Old Trafford. It seemed hours before the police let us cross Chester Road, and suddenly, there it was. The headlights embedded in the roof of the stand helped to conceal the stadium's glory until the last possible moment, the glistening red brick radiant against its sullen surroundings as the clicking turnstiles filtered off the ocean filling the vast forecourt.

'I'll see you after the game, darling.'

He gave me one of his my-little-son smiles, and I moved away abruptly in an effort to separate myself from him and the ill-ease it engendered. Once inside the ground with the programme in my hand, I felt I'd arrived. I examined its cover, the figures shaking hands, the number, the date, the fixture, just to make sure it really was happening, then ran up the steps of the stand, unable to wait any longer for my first view of the ground I'd seen so often on television. I was shocked by how much the sight of what was, after all, only a football pitch moved me, as I visualised the heroes and their exploits on the turf. It didn't matter that most had gone or that those who remained could never repeat their great deeds, that just lent the occasion poignancy, but as the teams ran onto the pitch and chants of 'U-NI-TED' rang round the ground, the football itself didn't seem to matter at all. I felt I belonged here as never before, as I joined in the singing, knowing I was as passionate about this club as anyone there. The state of the art electronic scoreboard read Manchester United o Tottenham Hotspur o. I hoped that would change soon. It did. When Martin Peters put Spurs one up, looking round, I noticed that Mecca had been infiltrated as about one hundred Spurs fans celebrated. A handful of United promptly steamed into them from the back of the Scoreboard End terrace, whacking a few before being arrested. Then Peters scored again, reducing the usually deafening Stretford End to the level of a village church congregation. I joined in the chants of 'You're gonna get your fuckin' 'eads kicked in', just to give myself a bit of a lift. By the time the referee blew his whistle, Peters had added two more. I had the compensation of seeing the great Bobby Charlton score, but this current team were just men. No mist swept round their feet as they left the pitch with their heads hanging after what turned out to be the worst home defeat of the season.

As Dad phoned his report through, the name Peters was polluting the press box air.

'Your team were lousy!'

He saw how dejected I was.

'Sorry about that,' he smiled sympathetically. 'Not much of a present.'

I felt bad. I remembered why I was there, and the pleasure it had given Dad to bring me to Old Trafford, but there was no way a fanatical United supporter could have enjoyed it. It was impossible to dissemble. I shrugged my shoulders.

In the pressroom I was introduced, with mutual disinterest, to several of his colleagues. Then a handsome, dark-haired man turned and gave Dad the warmest smile he'd yet received, and all the joy knocked out of me returned. Pat Crerand, one of the gods who looked down on me as I lay asleep at night, had stepped down from his picture. The pain when he squeezed my hand confirmed he was real.

'They could have done with you today, Paddy.'

'There's a lot happening here, Brian.'

'Do you think we'll stay up?'

I was surprised to hear myself speak.

'Of course, son. Just going through a bad patch.'

His words reassured me for a moment, but I'd seen enough to realise that the situation was dire.

Outside the ground the streets were dark and empty, strewn with bottles, cans, half-eaten burgers and torn-up programmes cast aside in disgust, but I felt good, bonded with Dad in a way

I hadn't been for a long time, part of his world. Although we discussed the game as equals, he felt more like a father than ever. On the journey home he reminded me of how alike we were. It was said with affection, inspired by the feelings that had been kindled in us both that day, but, like the smile he'd given me before I entered the ground, it seemed to imply ownership. I felt ambivalent about the prospect of turning into another version of him; on the one hand I was filled with admiration for a man apparently so successful professionally, financially and with women, on the other afraid that I might never achieve that success, and that if I did, I might, in that last respect, grow up to hurt someone as much as I felt he had my mother.

* * *

Beta was from Berlin; more confident and mature than most of our other au pairs, her English already very good. She'd been working as personal assistant to one of the editors in a German publishing house and now she would be cleaning ours. Where others faded at the court of King Brian, Beta flourished. Poking fun at Dad and quick enough to return fire in the nightly shoot-outs, she slipped into our family like a long-lost older sister.

One evening she failed to come down for dinner. Liz offered to look for her. Ten minutes later she was back.

'Beta's in floods of tears. She's really upset.'
'Did she tell you what's wrong?'
Mum looked anxious.
'She won't say.'
'You're very quiet, Brian. Anything the matter?'

'Nothing, mutteler. Okay kids, I'm going up to watch *Kojak*. Coming anybody?'

'Be nice if you stayed and helped with the washing-up for a change.'

'Why, dearest daughter, when I have four wonderful children?'

He picked several newspapers off a pile by his seat, and left.

'I'm going to see how Beta is.'

Liz followed Mum upstairs. By the time Mum returned I was alone, finishing the drying.

'Don't you want to see *Kojak*?'

She was scowling.

'Where's Liz?'

'Upstairs talking to Beta.'

She picked up a tea-towel and began drying the plates vigorously, as if she were wiping the nose of a petulant child.

'God, he makes me sick!'

'Who?'

My question was faux naïf.

'The poor girl's in a dreadful state up there. Your father tried to seduce her. He just can't control himself. Even shits on his own door-step.'

'He's done it before?'

Mum wrinkled her forehead. I knew the answer. My question had been prompted by a prurient fascination with the minutiae of Dad's indiscretions.

'Sylvia: I caught them snogging on the sofa. Fat lump of Swiss lard!'

I remembered Sylvia, bad-tempered and unfriendly with long black hair. I used to lift her skirt to see her knickers, which really irritated her. Now I was glad I'd humiliated her, but annoyed that while I was indulging in horseplay it appeared that Dad had been getting the real thing.

'What did you do?'

'I was furious with him.'

'What about her?'

'Oh, that silly tart! She didn't have long to go with us.'

'So you let her stay.'

'I needed help, Mark.'

'How could you after that?'

'I told Brian that if it ever happened again he'd be out.'

'So what's going to happen now?'

'I don't know.'

Mum began to sob uncontrollably and I gave her a big hug. I found it easier to cope when she was angry, but when she started to cry, I felt useless and angry at myself for not being able to be angry with Dad, but I so wanted her to stop. I stroked her back as she hugged me more tightly. There was a crack on the stairs. I didn't know what to say if Dad should catch us. But it was Liz, irate yet in control.

'He's a bastard.'

Mum broke out of our embrace.

'How's Beta?'

'She's very upset. The stupid fucker. Christ! He's so fucking immature. He just can't control himself. It's got nothing to do with you, Mum.'

'Of course it has!'

'It hasn't. He just has this constant need to prove that he's still attractive, but he loves you very much.'

'How can he?'

'Oh Mum, of course he does. You know that.'

For the next few weeks Dad's behaviour was as well groomed as his appearance. His stubble was only ever shaved when there was an attractive young woman in the house, but now he also seemed to have discovered a previously unsuspected flair for kitchen chores.

* * *

Any lingering family tensions evaporated in the warm sea air of the Adriatic. My parents had rented an isolated villa fifteen minutes from the resort of Fano, approached via a winding, mile-long mud track. I was sharing a room with Liz — and Beta who would parade round it in the morning, naked but for utilitarian white cotton pants. I'd heard that the doctors in our local surgery admired Beta's large nipples and now I could see why, although her breasts were as boyish as her underwear. I'd always be sure to remain in bed until she'd dressed, and watch her pull on her tantalisingly tight jeans.

Down on the beach the temptations were, if anything, greater. Firm bronzed flesh beckoned and winked. It was torture. The trouble was, at sixteen plus they were all a couple of years older than me, which didn't prevent the girls inviting me to the disco, but did disincline my parents from letting me go.

'They're interested in older boys. You'll only end up wretched.'

Each day the offer would be renewed. Each day I was forced to refuse, and while they discoed the dusk away I'd be lying in bed nursing a painful erection, Beta almost naked beneath the sheets in the bed opposite, my imagination rampant with visions of voluptuous Italian girls engaging in every conceivable form of sexual act with me.

To make matters worse, every day a sports car would negotiate the track beneath our house, veering off to a secluded, abandoned building in the abutting woodland with its booty. The female passenger was different each time, the driver the same. Our car making regular journeys was rendering the track almost impassable. Two would eventually lead to us having to be towed out by oxen – or so Dad reasoned. Next time the local Lothario's glinting silver car appeared, the males of the Glanville family marched on the intruder. Dad thumped on the only internal door long enough for trousers to be pulled up and skirts adjusted. A bearded man appeared, smiling amiably, and proffered his hand to be shaken in turn by all three of us.

'*Buon giorno. Sono il proprietario!*' (Good morning. I'm the owner.)

Looking at the decayed plaster, broken floorboards, exposed brickwork and glassless windows, the only response could be pity. Dad warned him he was rendering the road impassable and that the next time he saw him he would call the *carabinieri*, all in fluent Italian. We never saw him again. Toby and I went back later and booted a gaping hole in the door to his harem.

The region also fostered nobler forms of love. At Gradara castle we saw the room where Gianciotto Malatesta had supposedly murdered his brother and wife, Paolo and Francesca da Rimini, whose eyes and lips had met for the first and last time only an instant before the descending knife sent them to an endless embrace in the second circle of Hell. Dante was so moved by Francesca's account of their plight, an echo of his own unsatisfied love for Beatrice, that he fainted with grief and consigned the wronged assassin to Caina, the lowest circle of all. I bought a postcard of Rossetti's representation of the unhappy pair, their pre-Raphaelite hair flowing in an eternal, ethereal embrace, and promptly found my own Francesca on the beach. Pale amid the dark Italian girls, she was an Austrian with hair that twisted and tumbled down her back like Francesca's in the picture. An earthy naturalness made communication with the other girls easy, with or without language, but I felt that my heroine floated on a higher plane, and I could only watch from below, in love and awe, suffering an unrequited passion she knew nothing of. Zeffirelli's film of *Romeo and Juliet* had affected me the same way months previously. Devastated by the grief and suicide of Olivia Hussey's beautiful Juliet, I'd gone to the bottom of the garden in tears and made a rather half-hearted attempt to hang myself from the swing on a triangular piece of metal.

When frustration had turned to pain I stopped going to the beach, and fell back on my favourite pastime of combat with insects. By day I fought a colony of red ants that infested a crumbling, lime-painted wall; by night I'd chase the gigantic moths that batted against the polystyrene-tiled ceiling in the bathroom and frightened my sisters. It was whilst chasing one such creature with an oar that I first noticed the little walled town in the distance, across the sloping fields at the back of our villa. To my overwrought fourteen-year-old mind it gradually acquired almost magical properties; it was a place of tranquillity and happiness immured against the woes of the world I was currently living in. One afternoon

I persuaded Mum to stay behind while everyone else went to the beach, and walk there with me, cross-country, through the yellow wheat-fields to the enchanted city. After a while the sea appeared to our right, and the carbuncle coastal towns seemed safely distant. Reaching the town was the realisation of a fantasy, and knowing its name, to hold a powerful talisman. Novilara. It was only later I discovered that it was the town to which Gianciotto Malatesta had retreated after Paolo and Francesca's murder. Men in caps and waistcoats playing boules on a freshly concreted surface, spoke what sounded like a Spanish-riddled dialect, older and different from the language ten miles away on the coast. Drinking coffee here I could smell the beans as if for the first time, my senses heightened and sharpened, finally, above the fog that had recently clouded every thought and image.

The remaining days of the holiday were spent in Dorset, where the sober climate and landscape of south-west England soon washed away the blood and grime of the Marche. Lighted cigarettes pushed through the letterbox of our cottage in Kent had combined with the threat of a housing development on the village green to make us briefly second-home-less, but by selling the film rights to his novel *A Roman Marriage*, Dad bought a thatched cottage in Piddlehinton, whose Victorian and Jacobean buildings merged to give the impression of a cottage loaf. We soon discovered new favourite locations for walks and tea to replace the ones in Kent, but most of our activities now centred around the house itself, specifically the drawing room. During the mornings we'd read there in silence; in the afternoons perform short homemade plays (the curtains over the French windows formed an ideal backstage area); and after supper we'd sit in front of the log fire whose perspex guard threw back other-worldly reflections that were the perfect accompaniment to the ghost stories we read by the light of its flame, sipping martinis. Not that we needed the judges and knights that haunted the pages of Bram Stoker and Sheridan Le Fanu when we had our very own nun. Just as the poltergeist at home in London seemed to have been roused by the activity of small children, so the unfortunate novice might have been disturbed by the energy of frustrated adolescents. Each night Mum was roused from slumber by banging and thumping on the bedroom ceiling, above which lay a sleeping Toby. Concerned that he'd be woken, not to say petrified, by the racket, she visualised a cross and then burned it into the ceiling, so putting a stop to these antics. Toby slept blissfully through the ritual haunting and exorcism, as did everyone else. It was only a year or so later that we discovered why the house never appeared to have been touched by the cleaner during our long absences. 'It's 'arnted! I feel funny in there alone,' Mrs Rose informed us, sounding uncannily like one of the retainers that populated our fireside tales of the supernatural. 'Oh ye-eah! It's well known in the village. Nun used to live there, got pregnant. 'Anged 'erself up the-ere,' she explained, widening her eyes appropriately whilst indicating Toby's attic room.

No one seemed more disturbed by these events than Beta who was also the one that frightened most easily when the ghoul emerged from the wardrobe at the climax of a fireside reading. To Liz and Jo she was still the welcome older sister who took a share in these activities, but my attraction was growing with greater familiarity, and the slight swell of her breasts under a tight black polo-neck or the curve of her firm thigh in faded blue jeans distracted me even more than the sight of her nakedness had in Fano.

I began to wonder how far I could take things. Each evening she'd allow me to kiss her goodnight while she lay beneath the sheets, naked but for the white cotton pants I'd seen so much of in Italy, and let me run my hands under the bedclothes, right down her back, to her buttocks and thighs, her lips parting involuntarily as I did so. In my mind I allowed the action to develop, taking her tongue in my mouth, slipping my hand down her pants, sliding beneath the bedclothes and making love to her. She must have been aware that as I left her room each night my cock was straining against my pyjamas.

After one such foray I was standing in the bathroom, vainly attempting to pee whilst waiting for my alter ego to descend. Matters weren't helped by the proximity of the loo to the airing cupboard where I knew Beta's underwear was drying. There it stood, hovering in no man's land when Mum pushed the door open and walked in.

'Goodness! What an enormous genital!'

Not even being caught crucifying slugs or aroused in charge of pornographic magazines had prepared me for such a humiliation.

Next morning she took me aside.

'Can I have a word? Beta's been complaining. She says you keep groping her.'

My forehead felt on fire with embarrassment.

'What a bitch!'

'Well, is it true?'

'I suppose. She doesn't exactly offer any resistance.'

'I gather she was very provocative in Italy.'

'Really?'

'Liz says she spent the entire time parading round the bedroom half-naked. I'd call that provocative. You know, Mark, what you need is a damn good poke!'

I shouldn't have been shocked. While the nation was throwing up its hands in horror at the appearance of *The Little Red School Book* and its permissive morality and disregard for authority, Mum was out buying us all a copy – though she rather spoilt the gesture by adding her own editorial. In my annotated edition, the first sentence 'All parents are paper tigers' now read 'Some parents are paper tigers.' It sat on my bookshelf alongside *The Communist Manifesto*, *Das Kapital* and a host of other tracts and pamphlets the Soviet regime's heavy subsidy afforded to my pocket money. The *Guardian* published my letters extolling the virtues of the egalitarian comprehensive school system I was part of over the iniquitous, class-perpetuating private one I'd left, and I started producing *The Marksist*, a socialist monthly distributed round the family which included a news section with headlines like 'Dustmen's pay to rise above that of solicitors' in order to irritate my grandmother. I joined the Young Communist League, the youth wing of the Communist Party and the even more hardline International Marxist Group, but this was spiked when a representative turned up at Holland Park Avenue wishing to speak to Comrade Mark Glanville. Peering round the staircase, intrigued to see who had called so late I heard Dad inform my fellow traveller 'he's our son and he's in bed.' I forgave him not long after when it was discovered that the IMG had helped the IRA to set up a bomb factory in Kilburn. In *Man: A Critical Analysis*, a book whose title was as modest as its ambition, I attempted nothing less than an explanation of the origins of culture, religion and civilisation using sources as diverse as Schopenhauer, Freud, Marx, Wittgenstein, Melanie Klein, the Koran, Nietzsche and A.J. Ayer. Unable to live and play out in the world as I would like to have done, I internalised it, picked at it and analysed it with the blunted tools of ill-formed ideas.

'What's 'at you got in yer bag?' asked a classmate one day as I surreptitiously slipped a copy of Korstner's *Kant* into my briefcase during a science lesson.

'Kant.'

'Wor, Cunt! Let's 'ave a look!'

It was probably exactly what I should have been reading instead.

* * *

On my first outing with the Cockney Reds I was caught in no man's land. Struggling to lever myself out of the quagmire of pseudo-accademia, I turned up in a very unstreetwise brown velvet jacket, perfect for browsing in antiquarian bookshops, inappropriate on a train carrying one of the country's most feared crews of violent football hooligans. Their recent trip to Cardiff, with the most vicious fighting seen at a football match in years, had alerted the media, and the platform at Liverpool Street looked like a film set as the full armoury of BBC outside broadcasting descended.

Norwich was an all-ticket affair, and we didn't have the numbers to justify a special train, instead making do with four reserved carriages. Farmers and gentry quivered or bristled as chants of 'We have fits of mental violence' and 'Psycho aggro' rent the air. At last I was among the tribe of scarred, tattooed faces that had so long fascinated me. Finding a space, I was joined by two skinheads and their greasy-haired, pockmarked companion who clambered into the empty seats around me, pushing aside my legs as they did so. I smiled at the one with the hair. He glared back.

'You Uni'ed?'

''Course.'

''Cos this is a Uni'ed carriage.'

He looked at me in disgust, the way other passengers had been looking at them.

'Wha's that you go' in yer bag?'

'Sandwiches.'

'Gi' 's one!'

I hauled my plastic bag onto the table, but before I could open it they'd grabbed it and were delving in, pulling out Mum's carefully-wrapped packed lunch, and attacking the contents in a way that made Dad look like a finishing-school graduate.

'Pwoorach!'

The skinhead opposite spat the contents of a roll onto the table.

'Fack's that?'

'Taramasalata.'

'Sands like a fackin' disease!' remarked the one with hair, who appeared to be their leader.

'Yeah! Fackin' tastes like one an' all!'

The third one grabbed a banana and finished it in two bites. I made do with the remaining taramasalata roll as my can of lager went the way of the food.

They began discussing the camera crew and it turned out their leader had been interviewed.

'What did they ask you?' I inquired.

'Words . . . words. Words! Ha! Ha! Ha!'

Hamlet's response to Polonius.

The door to our carriage opened, and in walked a tall, bearded man with receding red hair. I recognised the brown pinstripe I'd seen him in at Euston on my first trip to Old Trafford. He moved through the carriage calmly, selling match tickets.

The bard was becoming agitated, 'If he facks me up I'm gonna whack 'im!' he growled, rocking back and forth, flashing venomous looks which I tried to avoid, staring fixedly at the flat East Anglian countryside whizzing past.

'I'll nick 'is fackin' ticket!'

Mum had supplied lunch, Dad the match ticket they knew I had. Catching glimpses of the ever-diminishing pile in the seller's hand I began to feel nervous. I was saved by a gentle 'Anyone here need match tickets?' and spent the rest of the journey looking out of the window, ignored by my fellow travellers and listening in to the conversation, which centred on their place of origin, Slough.

Inside the ground United had been allocated half the Barclay stand and were divided from the home fans by a low fence and the usual blue line. I was stuck in what was normally the away section, fenced off from our own fans by high cage wire put there to protect the generally much smaller followings of other clubs. Rumour had it that a United fan had been stabbed in Norwich the night before; not that any excuse was needed to attack the home fans. As the front line swarmed over the barrier and overwhelmed the police, the Norwich supporters fled and the cage dividing us from the other United fans rattled and shook under the weight of people scrambling up the wire, desperate not to miss out on the action. Amongst them I noticed the bard of Slough, grinning at his friends as he propelled himself, ape-like, upwards. Each time the police regrouped, United charged them again.

Worse was to come. United slumped to a 2–0 defeat, and while the Norwich fans mocked and celebrated, those around me unleashed whatever missile came to hand. This had entered a different league from anything I'd witnessed on the terraces of Loftus Road. No longer a velvet-jacketed academic on a day trip to Norfolk, I had become enthused by the same violent hatred as everyone else, and surged down the terrace towards a Norwich fan who was mouthing off at us from the adjacent stand, eyeballing him, threatening to carve his face open, certain I would if the chance arose. Everyone seemed engaged in violent activity of some sort or other. Civilised values were turned upside down in the vortex of hatred I'd become part of, and as I screamed and yelled, I felt as if my rage were pouring out of a bottomless well of anger, in a context where it was accepted, expected even, that one should threaten, fight, and destroy. At the end of the game, while the Norwich fans left as quickly as they could, United began to systematically destroy the stand, tearing down the corrugated iron at the back, then scaling up to the roof itself. Missiles blackened the air, some aimed at Norwich, some at the coppers, others at anything with glass in it. One fan fell thirty feet to the ground and was jumped on by incensed home supporters. When there was almost nothing left to pick off the former stand, the cohorts began to filter through the exit, past the heavily guarded home supporters who'd been kept in the forecourt. But the blood lust wasn't sated yet. Bottles, bricks, and other debris were hurled over the wall before the invading army finally made its way back to the trains and coaches, smashing the windows of the houses and shops en route. On the journey home there was a feeling of exhilaration as people compared their trophies – sheets of corrugated iron, fragments of pipe, lengths of guttering. I smiled at those around me through a blinding headache, hoping that the way it furrowed my brow might make me look hard, now we were away from the props and supports of the scene of our crime. Dad had seen it all on the news, and asked me for my version of events. But I found the patronising 'Marky darling's' that punctuated his enquiries intolerable, and swore at him.

'Ugh!' he responded, as though he'd been struck. 'You sound just like one of those pieces of filth you've been mixing with.'

I woke the following day with my head still throbbing painfully and feeling more depressed than ever. At the time I saw it as cold turkey, the reaction to being back in a world of sexual frustration and friendlessness. It didn't occur to me that the apparent catharsis of the dark vein I'd opened at Norwich had disguised the release of a lot of unpleasant feelings normally buried safely in my unconscious.

BBC Nationwide featured our exploits on the Monday. The government wasn't impressed and announced that United fans were to be excluded from all future away games, which now became all-ticket affairs for home supporters only. To my surprise, Dad was prepared to support my strange new pastime, as if the fix it had given me was preferable to certain even more unconscionable adolescent alternatives. Accordingly he called up Bristol City and bought me a ticket for the game at Ashton Gate a few weeks later. On this occasion I was determined not to make another sartorial slip-up, and turned up at Paddington in denim trousers and jacket and monkey boots, proudly sporting a Manchester United London Fan Club badge. Had I been wearing my bookshop-browsing attire, I wonder whether I would have attracted the attention of the ruddy-faced, fat middle-aged man in the opposite seat who spent the entire journey attempting to entwine his legs with mine. The assurance with which he pestered me was the clearest indication that my disguise as one of the famous football hooligans, part of an elite squad bound for Bristol in flagrant disregard of Government edicts was not yet perfected.

'I'm sorry if I've embarrassed you,' he lied as we approached Bristol Temple Meads, the unctuousness of his voice a nasty, oily substance I wanted to wash off as quickly as possible.

Inside the ground I was happy to see several hundred others had also beaten the ban. Today no United supporter could question my right to be there. I was one of the few to make it, an ultra-loyal Red. After the game we charged up a bank towards an open piece of ground to see if any Bristol were up for it, but it wasn't until we reached the narrow bridge over the Severn that it became interesting. Around two hundred of theirs had mobbed up on the other side of the river. I was worried we'd be picked off as we filed, singly, down the narrow iron steps. Bristol's mob was still about a hundred yards away, so there was enough time for the first fifty United to reach the other side. Without waiting to be asked, they charged at the superior numbers who, much to my relief, turned and ran back up the street. By Christmas, United, playing their best football since I'd been watching them, had only lost one other game, and looked set for a triumphant return to the first division.

* * *

If only Louise had come to me in reality, I might not have needed the outlet supplied by the Cockney Reds. In my dream we sat in silence at a table in the school library. All communication was through our eyes, hers sympathetic and protective, mine responding to the unifying bond of support and love that belonged to us, strong and unbreakable. She haunted me, in my mind when she wasn't in sight, but in reality I doubted she was aware of my existence. Each break-time brought another revelation of her beauty; her grape-black hair, curling and cascading, her eyes a transparent aquamarine, full, yielding lips, and a wide, almost African nose.

Mum had recently bought me a recording of Schubert songs, and I'd never heard anything more sublime. The tension of its romanticism straining to break through classical convention tuned me to the pitch of agony, which came in the form of Louise.

I think of you when the sun shimmers across the sea . . .
I see you in the dust that rises off the distant path . . .
I hear you in the running water . . .
The sun's sinking and the stars are rising. Oh were
  you here!

Like the lover in Goethe's 'Nearness of the Beloved' I perceived her in everything. As each day I moved farther from actuality into the dream of Louise, its flame burned stronger alongside my grief at the impossibility of its feelings ever metamorphosing into reality.

Fate had ordained that my new Francesca should be the daughter of one of the men who'd helped Dad found his amateur football team, Chelsea Casuals, twenty years before. I sat on the grass embankment opposite the ugly, oversized greenhouse of the school, clutching the black and white photograph Dad had lent me of the original Chelsea Casuals team, propped and lolling in the mud like turn of the century Old Etonians. In the picture Dad was twenty-five; it was just before he met Mum. It was a quarter of an hour till the end of lunch. I'd wasted forty-five minutes trying to glimpse her through her surrounding veil of friends. Break would be over in five minutes. My stomach twisted with anxiety. Although she was only twenty yards away, she might as well have been in India. I feared by the time I reached her she'd have vanished as surely as she had when I woke from my recurrent dream. In a way I almost hoped she would, but she was still there, her handmaidens parting to make way for me. Any inspiration was dragged under by the weight of my overly premeditated manoeuvre.

'Hi.'

'Hi.'

I was making more impact on her watching circle. Out came the photo.

'Have you seen this?'

'No.'

'Both our Dads are in it.'

'Aha.'

I weighed her interjection.

'Can you see your Dad?'

She identified him immediately.

'Can you guess which one is mine?'

This was the closest I'd come to a chat-up line. She

pointed him out as swiftly and accurately as she had her own.

'You know they both used to play in the same team, Chelsea Casuals?'

'I know.'

She could only have known because at some stage she'd discussed the fact, so perhaps she was interested in me.

'They founded it in 1956.'

It would have been hard to find anything more prosaic to say. The pips went for the end of break and my chance with them. I learned nothing about her in the course of our brief exchange, but she'd seen that I was gauche, unconfident and hardly a worthy suitor.

I started to identify more and more with the lovelorn hero of Schubert's song cycle *Die Schone Mullerin*, whose experience seemed to mirror my own. Just as in the song cycle, any remaining tranquillity was shattered by the arrival of the huntsman, in the form of a classmate bolder and more assured than me, and I watched in pain and disbelief as my angel was brought to earth.

The verses of Catullus helped sublimate my pain. While the girls who made up the rest of my Latin 'O' level class fretted when he suggested that the words of an amorous woman should be written on the wind or running water, I was looking for texts that would prevent me from drowning myself in the brook, like Schubert's wretched hero. (I regularly took knives and razors to the backs of my arms, but fortunately lacked the inclination and courage to apply them to my wrists.) Catullus' poems spoke to me; his experiences echoed my own.

I found my situation most sympathetically reflected in his version of a poem by the Greek writer Sappho:

> *He seems to me like a god*
> *(If it's possible, better)*
> *Who sits beside you, looks at you*
> *And hears your sweet laughter.*
> *But in my misery it tears my senses apart,*
> *For as I look at you nothing is left to me.*
> *My tongue is numb, a subtle flame licks my limbs,*
> *My ears ring with their own sound,*
> *Both my eyes are blinded by night.*

The Latin translation made me curious to read the Greek original, and it wasn't long before I'd discovered Oxford's 'Greats' degree course, which would allow me to indulge my growing passion for Latin and Greek literature as well as my more established enthusiasm for philosophy. The course became my holy grail, and at first seemed as tangible. At Pimlico Latin had never been taught beyond 'O' level, nor had a single curling, accented line of Homer and his ilk ever graced the books that clogged its store cupboards, but I was persistent, and David Thornley, a polyglot Spanish teacher, kindly agreed to cram in a couple of Greek lessons a week during his precious breaks, along with a weekly ancient History tutorial and an 'A' level Latin session to supplement the couple of official ones I received.

As I was the only pupil, I was assigned a store cupboard at the end of the concourse, close to where my nose had been fractured. It was more lawless there than ever. As we sat in our cell one day, knees bumping together beneath a passage of

Plato, glass-shattering riots were taking place just outside the thin, cardboard-padded door. After waiting the sensible five minutes we peered out of our cubbyhole. All of the windows in sight were broken, even the heavy, wire-reinforced stuff in the firebreak doors. Everyone knew who it was – a local gang – some students at the school, that had recently been involved in a series of sharpened comb and machete confrontations with a West Indian posse from Brixton at the school gates. I was given a key so I wouldn't have to linger in the badlands, although it wasn't long before the headmistress was forced to employ security guards to patrol the concourse. I was usually unperturbed when I did encounter loitering drug-dealers and gang members. I likened myself, proudly, to King Charles in *L'Allouette*, the Anouilh play I was studying for 'A' level, who confronts and conquers his timidity after being assured by Joan of Arc that true courage is not to be found in the boar who hurtles into perilous situations without a thought, but in those with imagination and sensitivity who succeed in overcoming their fear in similar circumstances. My bogeymen weren't bishops and generals, but whoever might be waiting for the Cockney Reds on a Saturday afternoon.

* * *

Would West Ham show? Five months previously we'd suffered our most humiliating terrace defeat at Upton Park as thousands of their finest swarmed down on us from the back of the South Bank, forcing us onto the pitch to avoid being whacked and crushed. The media had it wrong as usual, perceiving the pitch invasion as a deliberate attempt to stop the game in the face of defeat.

All the faces turned out for the return. I found an empty carriage and took potluck. Moments later I heard boots thumping down the corridor and excited voices. My door slid open.

'Anyone sittin' 'ere, mate?'

There were three of them. A half-caste with an earring in a leather bomber-jacket seemed to be the leader. I'd seen him around but I didn't recognise his companions, a black guy with an Afro and a stocky, blond bloke with acne. They all looked as if they could handle themselves. I quickly shoved my copy of the *Guardian* down the side of the seat.

''Ere, Tiger, see 'is fackin' face?'

'Yeah, bang!' Tiger threw a punch at a phantom boxer and laughed.

'Never seen no one go dan so fast.'

'"We'll fuckin' 'ave you!" Ha! Ha! Ha! Yeah, like fack!'

'Who was it?' I asked.

'West 'am.'

'Oh, they showed.'

'Nah. Jus' one geezer. Don' reckon they've got the bo'lle after what 'appened. You wait till Piccadilly. 'Ole of Salford'll be there.'

'So where're you blokes from, then?'

''Ang on a minute, mate, an' I'll show yer.'

As the train slowed out of Euston, they were on their feet.

'Right. See over there? Them big tower blocks? That's where we live.'

He sounded proud of the urban desolation he was pointing at.

'Bes' fackin' mob in norf Landon!'

'I believe you.'

'Do yer?'

The lines on his brow deepened. They looked as though they'd been etched by a carpet knife, and for a moment I was afraid that he might have interpreted my response as piss-take rather than affirmation.

'No, you really believe me? Two 'andred fackin' top boys. 'Ard that estate is, fackin' 'ard. You don' live there otherwise. Wha' abaht you. Where you from?'

'North Ken.'

'What, North Kemp? You mus' 'ave a long way to cam.'

'Nah. North Kensington. You know. Notting Hill, Ladbroke Grove.' I cited the hinterland behind Holland Park Avenue. His eyes lit up and he started listing people he knew in the area, none of whom would have shopped at my local delicatessen.

'Still. Mus' 'ave some good laughs though. 'Ere, Bill. 'Ad a laugh las' night, didn' we? We was in this chippy, an' this fackin' Mick looks at Bill like 'e wants to do somethin' abah' it, so when 'is chips cam, Bill pulls the vinegar aht 'is 'and, an' sprinkles it in 'is eyes. "Oy! Gosh! Begorrah! Fockin' Jesus," an' 'e looks up an' Bill nuts 'im, dincher, Bill?'

''At's right. Baff! Righ' on 'is fackin' Paddy nose. I 'eard it crack, then it went all soft like, an' then 'is blood's fackin' everywhere, all over 'is chips. Ha! Ha! Like tomato fackin' ketchup. But the cunt's go' it all over me jacket . . .'

'So Bill says "'Ere, Paddy! You gonna do somethin' aba' it? 'Ow 'm I gonna explain this to me missus?" So 'e reaches over the coun'er, grabs a Coke bottle. Bang! bang! bang! Dan on the Paddy's 'ead, so the cant's lyin' on the floor so I stamps on 'is 'ead, boof! boof! An' then Bill treads on 'is bollocks. Fer good measure, like.'

Tiger roared with laughter, anxious features momentarily beatified by the events he was describing. The black guy was shaking in his seat, Bill laughing chestily. I adjusted my jaw into a rictus, and felt the onset of a violent headache. I couldn't contribute, only listen. Even if I'd been able to match their narrations, I couldn't have simulated the relish with which they recounted them, so I let them talk, and tried to fix my expression into admiration rather than horror.

''Ere, mate. Wha's your name, by the way?'

I was embarrassed by the surge of warmth that went through me.

'Mark.'

'Yeah, Mark, ask Denz ter tell yer abah' wha' we dan at the school.'

'What happened, Denz?'

'Our ol' school, las' week right, we broke in, right, an' we was gonna torch it, weren' we Tiges? Then we goes to our ol' classroom an' we throws all the desks over the floor . . .'

'An' Denz pulls 'is trousers dan an' done this big turd right on the teacher's fackin' desk. Din'cher, Denz?'

'Tha's right. A great, big brown steamin' one. Hur! Hur! Bet she were well surprised next mornin'!'

'Yeah, Denz! You fackin' shitter! Ha! Ha! Anyway. I've been ap since 'alf five an' I need a kip.'

With that, Tiger levered himself onto the luggage net above the seat while the others shut the curtains over the door and windows and unscrewed all the light bulbs. Denz took the other hammock and Bill the seat opposite me. I wasn't tired but at least under cover of darkness my jaw could relax, and I could smile as myself, flushed with a strangely pleasurable, if illicit, sensation of acceptance.

Before the train had finished pulling into Manchester Piccadilly, most of its contents had already hit the platform and were running towards the ticket barriers chanting the Cockney Red war cry, heads twisting from side to side, taking in the possibilities. Outside the station, Tiger seemed to know where he was heading, so we followed him down the dingy Victorian alleyways and narrow side streets until he stopped at what looked like a cave carved out of the wall, protected by reinforced steel double doors and two hippopotami in jeans and T-shirts who adjusted their snarls and nodded us through. We walked down a poorly lit tunnel that juddered with the bass from a jukebox pumping out 'Magic Fly' in satanic counterpoint with ritual chanting that rose as if from Hades. Once past another set of double-doors we were at the heart of the place. Gaunt, expressionless skinheads with scarred cheeks and freshly blackened eyes squatted or stood in the dark, smoky room, filling the air with the fag smoke they exhaled like a synchronised dry ice machine.

'Brummie Reds we are here . . .'

'Boston Reds we are here . . .'

'Salford Reds we are here, shag your women and drink your beer!'

'They don't like Cockneys in 'ere,' warned Denz, 'so don't talk too much.'

I finished my first pint in twenty seconds.

'Cor! You didn'arf dan that one fast!' exclaimed Tiger. ''O wants anuvver?'

The others were barely past the froth, but not to be outdone they emptied their glasses swiftly. I finished my second in about the same time.

'You carn 'arf fackin' put 'em away!' remarked Tiger

admiringly. ''Ere, you oughta cam ter Belgium wiv us next month, ter the beer festival. We 'ave a right laugh. Shoulda seen Denz las' year. 'E were lyin' face dan in the bogs covered in spew an' some cunt cam an' pissed all over 'im. It was fackin' 'ysterical!'

I laughed, but my mirth was interrupted by the whiz of a heavy glass ashtray flying past my right ear. I glanced round nervously for any Cockney-haters and was relieved to see that the target was, in fact, sitting behind me. He hurled it back, and for a while the air was thick with missiles. Then a bovver-booted suedehead walked over to the original victim and nutted him in the face, with enough force to make him lose his balance and fall between the chairs and the table. As the curly-haired victim lifted his head, someone else slapped him hard round the side of the face.

'We want Bonzo as our leader, 'cos e's big an' fuckin' daft!'

They poured beer over his head, then put their arms around each other and started singing 'Boston Reds we are here . . .' But this was just horseplay. I wondered what they'd be like in a proper fight.

'D'yer 'ear abaht them City wot cam an' 'ave a go dan 'ere a coupla weeks ago?' asked Tiger. ''Baht fifty of 'em. Chased 'em all over Piccadilly Gardens. Murdered the cants!'

There was to be no such excitement today. Although we won 4–0, everyone was disappointed that West Ham hadn't shown. Where were the South Stand boys when the odds were against them?

It wasn't long before Tiger and his gang became the closest thing I had to a circle of friends. I told myself that the special trains pulled into Euston too late for me to make the regular weekend parties held by my classmates. The truth was I hadn't been invited. In the sixth form at Pimlico I was a total outsider, unable and unwilling to take part in endless bewilderingly passionate debates about Led Zeppelin, Genesis and Cream, or in laddish story-swapping of sexual experiences I hadn't had, no doubt because I couldn't talk about rock music. At break I sat alone, willing the clock to tick faster. My passions for classical music, ideas, literature, even reggae, isolated me, made me feel as much a pariah as the football hooligans who gave me their odd friendship on match days. Frightening as their violence was, I was drawn by the outlaw status I felt I shared with them.

* * *

But for my next train journey I was back in velvet jacket and tie, desperately trying to remember how I'd answered the questions on my Oxford general paper, more janglingly nervous than I had been approaching Euston the night the Millwall special had overtaken us at Milton Keynes.

'Mr Glanville, if I may refer to your answer to the question "In what way may Virgil's *Aeneid* be considered a civilised epic?" You say, and I quote, "You can tell how uncivilised Homer is from the table manners of the Cyclops." What did you mean by this?'

The professor of Greek History put his hands on his knees and laughed, the Philosophy Fellow, who'd spent the entire time reading *The Times* behind a snooker table continued to do so, while the Classics Fellow waited for an answer to his question.

'Well it isn't very civilised, dashing people's brains out against a cave wall then swallowing them whole.'

I left Wadham certain I wouldn't be returning. The following day I was summoned to Pembroke, my third-choice college.

'Mr Glanville, what could I say that would really excite you?'

Austere though his manner, unexpected his question, the Ancient History tutor looked so like Benny Hill's straightman, I found it hard to take him seriously, even when he informed me that my Latin language paper was shocking.

Two weeks later, to my enormous surprise and delight, Pembroke offered me a place. As a reward Mum took me to see *Eugene Onegin* at Covent Garden, and a few days later I sang a few bars of Prince Gremin's declaration of love to my old clarinet teacher, Marjorie, whom I still saw from time to time. She raced to the piano and asked me to sing some scales and arpeggios, exclaimed 'You've got a voice!' and promptly got on the phone to a singer friend.

Back home I hauled out every record with a tune I knew and sang along. Marjorie's friend heard me, approved, and recommended a distinguished former lieder singer called Mark Raphael. I went for a consultation at his home in St John's Wood. A tiny, bald man, no more than 5′ 2″, answered the door.

'Mark Raphael?' I pronounced his name like the angel's.

'Rayful, my dear, Rayful.'

He had the authority of a man a foot taller. His articulation was impeccable, with just a hint of an old East-London Jewish accent. The room into which he'd ushered me testified to the career he'd had, its walls and mantelpiece decorated with pictures of him shaking hands with the great accompanist

Gerald Moore, and arm in arm with Gigli. Watching over the proceedings, arms folded, was a large portrait of the singer as a young man. I was in awe. He led me down a short flight of steps to his studio, a long, extended room with a grand piano by the entrance, music lining the front half, books, including an impressive collection of English poetry, the back.

'What have you brought me, my dear?'

His brown eyes shone behind glasses that bestrode a classic Jewish conk. I started Schubert's 'Aufenthalt', a dramatic song in which the poet likens his dwelling place to the turbulent natural elements that reflect the angst in his soul. I'd listened to it when feeling particularly tortured by unrequited love for Louise, and I knew what I wanted to express, but my voice was unequal to my intentions. Mark frowned.

'I think I heard something.'

That was enough. I started having regular lessons, which I enjoyed as much for Mark as the music.

'Don't you think Schubert's the composer closest to God?'

'No, my dear. He's the composer closest to Earth.'

'Schmaltz! More schmaltz! They used to ask Richard Tauber why he was so popular and d'you know what he said? It's because I've got sex in my voice. Sex, sex, sex!' he arpeggioed, breaking into the aria 'Bella siccome un angelo', moving his right leg up and down as he accompanied himself, like some naughty satyr.

We decided it would be good for me to spend some time in the homeland of opera, so I signed up for a six-week singing course in Siena which I could attend as an observer. I'd just turned eighteen, and this would be my first solo venture abroad. I nervously saw myself stumbling through Italy like a drunk across an unfamiliar room, reaching in desperation for any object that might stop my fall; in this case it was the many friends and acquaintances Dad had there. I spent my first evening off the Transalpine train with David, an American composer who'd diagnosed Dad's tuberculosis where doctors had failed to see anything. Drunk on young chianti, I returned to the Bartolini Pensione in which Dad had convalesced twenty-five years before. Depositing my bags there earlier, I'd been shocked by the coldness of my reception from the shrivelled padrona of Dad's youth, but worse was about to follow. She opened the door and glared at me.

'The door to your bedroom. You 'ave broken eet.'

I was led like a naughty schoolboy to a room I'd scarcely even made acquaintance with.

'Look!'

She flopped the handle up and down like an impotent penis.

''Ow you open eet?'

I pushed the handle down.

'No!'

She pulled the handle up with an exasperated sigh.

'You must pay for eet.'

'Is there anywhere I can sleep?'

She shrugged and turned wearily, like a prison warder forced to lead a child-murderer to a new cell.

It was larger than the original, but its most noticeable feature was the height of the ceiling on which had assembled what looked like a regiment of the Arno's finest mosquitoes. I did battle all night and by morning had achieved a Pyrrhic victory – the recent red splotches on the walls and ceilings equalling the large yellow welts on my face and body.

I turned up for my singing course in Siena exhausted, but
found what appeared to be a haven: my bedroom had views
across the Tuscan farmlands, in a family house tucked away
in a square dominated by one of the gigantic white-stuccoed
churches that serve the *contradas* whose horses compete in
the annual *Palio*. It didn't take me long to realise that the
tranquillity was only an illusion. Even the signora's welcoming
wine couldn't drown out the drum-rolling parades rehearsed
in the Club della Giraffa below me all afternoon, or the noisy
conversation that carried on there until four each morning.
When I complained, the signora's son promised to buy
ear-plugs, 'For a friend! I buy them for you as a friend!'
and embraced me.

The course was held at the Academia Chigiana, a medieval
palazzo, where Maestro Favaretto (according to David, Tuscan
for little prick) smiled benignly at the eager Japanese girls
who comprised 90% of the class. Afterwards I went to the
Café della Fonte Gaia on David's instructions, 'It's where the
young things sniff each other's crotches!' They didn't, but it
was pleasurable to sit and watch the ease with which the
six-hundred-year-old square accommodated the posture and
dress of its latest occupants, like everywhere in Italy, just as
happy to be lived in as admired. On returning to my room I
found that my wallet, containing all the money I owned, was
missing. Taking advice from yet another of Dad's friends, I
went to the police and issued a denuncia against my hosts.

'*Siamo molto Cattolici. Guarda! Una Madonna qua, una Madonna
la. Che vergogna!*' (We're very Catholic. Look! A Madonna here,
a Madonna there. What shame!) wept the signora, who later
confided that her son hadn't been the same since a serious car
accident. I left Tuscany the following day, chiefly because I

seemed to be courting disaster wherever I went there, but also because there seemed little to be gained from watching Maestro Favaretto flattering obsequious young Oriental women.

Another old friend of Dad's, a football manager called Biti, invited me to stay with his family in an apartment just outside the centre of Rome. He was away training a new club, but his wife, a large woman, whose blonde, scraped-back hair was tinged world-weary grey, served me the largest bowl of pasta I'd ever seen in my life, while her daughter, Paola, became my Virgil, escorting me to all the tourist sites locals never normally visit. After the suffocating medieval provincialism of Florence and its narrow gridlock, Rome's broad, light-filled streets, no matter how traffic-laden, were an oxygenating joy.

Against Paola's wishes we went to St Peter's and the Vatican.
'Everything you see here is taken from somewhere else. So much wealth. It is disgusting.'
It was refreshing to hear a Catholic raging against a church I'd not exactly been brought up to love either.
'I am not a Catholic. I was brought up as a Catholic.'
I enjoyed Paola's companionship. It was a relief after the hostility I'd experienced in Tuscany, but one day her frankness took me aback.
'I think you are a cold person.'
'I'm English.'
'But I know other English people, and they are warm.'
At first I was hurt, but then I began to wonder whether she hadn't said this because I'd somehow, unwittingly, hurt her.
'In what way am I cold?'
'I think maybe you study too much. In England do you have many friends?'

'I don't have time.'

I didn't tell her I made sure I never did have, because if I did it would give me the space to reflect on why I was so lonely.

Paola liked doing things in groups. I started to feel jealous of the friends who occupied the hours I could have been spending with her. One weekend she took me to Ostia. There was barely a towel-space to be found between the packed thousands of escaping Romans grilling on the sandy strip between the beach and the road. Paradoxically this was the nearest we'd come to being alone, here in the midst of the anonymous hordes. As we left the beach and headed for Ostia Antica, Paola slipped her arm through mine and smiled at me, and it was as if a veil had been lifted. For the first time I noticed how the ochre of her skin set off the crystal blue of her eyes, the slimness of her nose and her bobbing, copper-coloured hair so unEnglish and exotic.

After the writhing populousness of the beach, Ostia Antica's desert spaces were a relief, but it was hard-going in such heat, and, as in the Forum, it was difficult to imagine the beauty and vitality of what had once been in the present de Chirico landscape.

'All the statues you see, they are not originals. The Vatican has taken them. Everywhere it is the same. They have stolen from the whole country.'

'And abroad.'

'Exactly.'

Let the virile youth learn
To suffer squeezing poverty as a friend

78

And may he be a thorn
In the side of the savage Parthians,
Feared for his spear, passing his life
Beneath the open heaven in terrifying conditions . . .
It is a sweet and fitting thing to die for one's country

That evening I sat on my bed reading Horace's Roman odes, hoping their bombast would help my imagination to clothe the ruins of the city and that, in turn, Rome's living presence might humanise the poetry. Paola came in, sat beside me and began to dry her hair.

'I do not want to disturb my mother. She is tired, *molto, molto stanca*,' she smiled. I froze; my excitement was overcome by anxiety that I mightn't be able to accomplish what I felt was now expected. I could barely admit it — even to myself — but I'd never kissed a girl properly before, not even Beta. Paola removed the Horace from my hands.

'Always studying,' and suddenly it was all being done for me. Her tongue was in my mouth, the smell of her freshly washed hair intense in my nostrils. I pushed her tongue back with mine and massaged her lips with my own, competing to see whose tongue could go in farthest. She separated from me, panting for breath. I panicked that she might have changed her mind, but then she smiled and leaned in again. She started to unbutton her shirt, then mine, moving her hand across my chest while I struggled with the metal rivet at the top of her jeans. Paola frowned and I thought I'd done something wrong, but then she kissed me again, passionately, and between us we managed to undress ourselves. I'd waited so long for this but now it was happening I was unaroused, and as I felt her open her legs beneath me I was somewhere else, detached from what was happening, willing myself to harden as if by telekinesis.

'I think you have not done this many times before.'

'I'm sorry.'

'Why? It does not matter. We have so much time.'

Not enough. At three in the morning Paola tiptoed out of the room I'd appropriated from her and slipped into bed beside her mother.

'*Paola, non ti hai vergogna?*' (Aren't you ashamed?)

We took the traditional path of most Italian youth and found places to make love al fresco, under trees, behind bushes. Beautiful as it was, for me the Roman summer sky lacked aphrodisiac properties. I enjoyed the closeness, the affection, but not the sex, even on the rare occasions when Signora Biti was out and we had the luxury of a bed. I'd overcome impotence but not the next hurdle. To my frustration and her chagrin I was unable to climax. Paola began to take it as a personal insult but the more I strove to reach my goal, the further it receded.

We returned one evening after yet another unsuccessful foray to find Il Mago del Tyrrheno (The Tyrrhenian Wizard) himself, eating pasta from my bowl. Paola's father had been shaping his new third-division side down at Formia, which I only knew as the site of Cicero's tomb. He was completely bald, with the tanned complexion of a man who spends his life outdoors. I wondered if he knew what was going on between his daughter and me. After the usual exchange of pleasantries I was given an impromptu trial in the living room. Biti chucked me a cloth ball which I controlled on my chest and volleyed at the door.

'Ha! Your balance is not right. See, if you strike the ball with your right foot you should hold out your left arm. Your brother does this right.'

The comment stung. Toby had had a trial for Formia as a result of which Biti had offered him a youth team contract. Although I was glad to have escaped the burden of Dad's sporting ambitions Toby was forced to carry, I'd have loved to inspire the pride my brother did. I could see the pitfalls of his position, the danger he might be realising Dad's dreams rather than his own, but then I stopped to think about it. Wasn't I too playing on my father's stage, out there in Italy, pretending I was independent when I was being fed and supported by his friends? I'd even lost my virginity to the daughter of one of them. Maybe that had been stage-managed too.

It was Paola's last night in Rome before a Sardinian camping holiday. Biti had gone and his wife given up her pretence at morality, so we could spend the night together, but it was more unsatisfying than usual.

'I'm sorry. I feel desexualised. I have done since I've been here,' I finally confessed.

'So why did you do this to me?'

'What?'

'If you are desexualised why did you allow this to happen? Do you think it's fair? Every day we are making love. Tomorrow I go and now you tell me all the time you feel desexualised. So why did you start it?'

'Paola, you did.'

I was as off balance with her as I had been with her father.

'Hah! And you had no interest at all?'

'Of course I did. I really wanted you.'

She raised her palms heavenwards in exasperation and left.

Our parting the following day in the presence of Signora Biti was as chaste as our initial greeting and I tormented myself, wondering if it would have been different had we been alone. I left for England the following day. Rome wouldn't be the same without Paola and I was behind on my reading with only a few weeks to go before the start of my first term at Oxford. In London I felt lonelier than ever, dreading immersion in a monastic, scholarly existence. Every time I stopped to look up the commentary on a passage of Euripides or Horace I could see Paola's face staring at me, its disappointment compounding my own sense of failure.

* * *

At least I had an outlet with the Cockney Reds. Fate had ordained that my last game before heading for Oxford would be a derby with hated City. I was a little unsure how I could explain my imminent absence to Tiger and co., but before I had the chance I was separated from his crew and ended up with Elly, an occasional Cockney Red who'd attach himself to whichever group or firm had left an empty seat in the carriage and didn't object too strongly to his piss-sodden odour. 5'9" in a scruffy, grey duffel coat, jeans and filthy trainers, he looked as though he'd never bathed voluntarily. Matted, mouse-coloured hair stuck to his forehead, framing a pitted, mongoloid face.

City's insipid sky-blue shirts headed towards the goal to our right and the whole paddock surged forward, chanting 'Fuck off City! Fuck off City!' eyes burning, and faces lined in loathing. The Old Bill hauled a few Rod Stewart clones out of the ground, their long hair making them soft targets.

I was barely making the game out through a five-pint haze when I heard the wooden terrace thunder beneath the weight of Elly's flying piss. People alerted in K-stand to our right wished they hadn't been.

'So, you goin' ter the game next week?' he asked me, tool in hand, quite unembarrassed.

'Nah.'

'Why's 'at then? Goin' on 'oliday?'

'Wish I was.'

'You goin' inside?'

At first I was shocked by the nonchalant manner in which he'd suggested this, and what that implied about him, his view of life and me. Then I realised he'd handed me the perfect get-out, one that would explain my long absence whilst allowing me to maximise my credibility, so I nodded with an assumed air of resignation and hang-dog look.

'What for, don' min' me askin'?'

'Manslaughter,' I replied lazily.

Elly stumbled, nearly slipping on the piss with which he'd coated the terrace around him.

'What, you? I can't believe it. You always seemed like a sort of m-mild geezer ter me. But you can't never tell!' He looked at me nervously. 'Them's often the ones! It's the quiet ones!'

'I didn't mean to.' A complete scenario had been developing in my head. 'I was just coming out of this club an' a bloke comes up and says I went off with his missus. I tried to walk away but the geezer pulls me round an' I thought he was going to hit me so I belted 'im, he staggers back, bangs his head against a lamp post, falls on the deck. Next thing I know he's dead and there's Old Bill everywhere. I never meant it.'

Elly looked almost as horrified as I was feeling at the ease with which my fabrication had unfolded.

''Ow long you reckon, then?'

'Dunknow. Brief reckons four years.'

That would see me nicely through Oxford.

In my enthusiasm to convince Elly I'd failed to notice that Joe Jordan had scored and we embraced each other. I was pungently reminded of how malodorous and piss-sodden he was, and shouldered past him and into the maelstrom of hugging fans surging between the crush-barriers. In flowed the Filth, grabbing people by the hair, whacking them, dragging them away. Some tried to pull the coppers off their mates, throwing miscued punches, only to be nicked themselves.

'We are the Scoreboard, the Scoreboard Paddock!' we chanted defiantly.

Reality impinged with the dart I saw sticking out of a City fan's head. 'One hundred and eighty!' someone shouted.

I was surprised not to see any City outside the ground. They hadn't been kept in. I clicked through the turnstile and made my way over the cracks of the station platform. Red and white wherever I looked. No action in the offing. I spotted a Cockney Red I knew by sight and went over to have a word. A good 6′ 3″ in his twenty-four-eyed Docs, Lofty always wore an old-fashioned crombie and kept his jet-black hair Mod-length.

'Great to beat those twats, eh?'

Lofty nodded.

'Great goal, Jordan!'

Lofty nodded. The train pulled in. Everyone charged aboard, as if it were the last helicopter out of Phnom Penh. We were among the first and piled onto the nearest seat. Three carriages miraculously absorbed the contents of the platform. One dirty, blue-jeaned backside was inches from my face, and the scrunched up programme in its back pocket played tag with my nose. As we bumped slowly towards Oxford Road, I stretched my neck to see beyond the bums and legs to the cheap jumpers and acne-covered faces of what I guessed, nervously, were the elusive City fans. A lone chant of 'We hate Man U' started somewhere to my right, testing the water. By the time it crescendoed to 'We are the Man U haters,' most of the carriage seemed to have joined in. I kept my face down to avoid eye contact, and tried to block out the situation by donning a mental tarnhelm.

'There's one over there! That coont, I've seen 'im before. 'E's one of them cockney twats. Oy! Foocking cockney coont! We'll foockin' 'ave you!'

It wasn't me. He'd recognised Lofty. Fortunately the weight of the people didn't allow for much movement, but that didn't deter this ginger-stubbled psycho. His first kick parted the crowd and missed Lofty by inches. The bloke in front of me tried to hold him down and make it easier next time, so I hauled him off by his hair and as I did so, Ginger hoisted himself onto the luggage racks and delivered his first successful blow, catching Lofty on the side of the head. We were heavily outnumbered, and in the packed carriage those trying to avoid the fight were getting in the way of the ones who wanted to join in. The bloke I'd pulled off Lofty tried to nut me, but I moved in time and his head caught the wooden panel behind, allowing me to deliver three quick hooks to his face. Lofty was coming off worse, although his assailant seemed too immersed in his Tarzan impression, swinging back and forth from the luggage racks like a bad-tempered gibbon, to be bothered about GBH, and then, suddenly, we were at Oxford Road. There was a roar as the toothpaste squeezed out of the tube. Two or three gave us final kicks and punches as they left the train while we huddled on the seat with our arms wrapped round our heads. Then the train began to move out of the station and we scrambled for the door before realising it was going on to Piccadilly.

Lofty and I grinned at each other. It was an intense thrill to have held our own against superior numbers and escaped a nasty beating; rather like a visit to the dentist's, the experience had turned out to be a lot less unpleasant than imagined. Lofty caught me looking at the deep gash over his right eye.

'Third fackin' time! Once in the Kippax, an' they done me dan Deansgate.'

He lifted his Ben Sherman shirt to reveal a two-inch scar above the ribs.

'That's where I got stabbed.'

On the train back I found Tiger and co. sitting in an open carriage with Banana Bob and a couple of the other top boys.

'It can fackin' sting!'

'Yeah. See these?' Bill pointed to his trainers. 'Now a pair of these in the face is more like an ache. You ever been dan by a pair of these?'

'Nah. But I'm tellin' yer mate, baseball boots fackin' sting.'

A massive, thickset bloke in a long, grey trench coat, face

as red as his hair, jabbed the air with his finger. It looked as if Bill was about to see his theories put to the test.

'You'd be surprised, mate. DM's ain't that bad.'

'You're jokin', aincher?' interjected Tiger, stamping on an imaginary head.

'Nah, you thick cunt! I mean this,' said the redhead, converting from forty yards.

'What? You tellin' me these ain't worse?'

'Yeah, I mean, I've 'ad me jaw broken, me nose broken by 'em, bu' it don' 'urt like baseball boots.'

'You're 'avin' a laugh, incher? 'Course it fackin' 'urts more. You fackin' two bob!'

Bill was having none of it.

'What about these?' I indicated my feet, more confident of my status than I should have been.

'What're them?' asked the redhead with almost pitying disdain.

'Monkey boots.'

'You're 'avin' a laugh, incher? Pair o' these in the face an' you'd fackin' know abah' it!'

He pointed at his ugly, square-toed black shoes.

'Dan a Leeds cant with these. Shoulda seen 'im, eye all split open, angin' out like a fackin' grape. Ha! Ha! Nose flat like a nigger's 'n' I reckon 'e mus' a' swaller all 'is teeth. 'E were rockin' back 'n' forth makin' this gurglin' noise, blood every-where. Take that you Yorkshire cant! Ha! Ha! Ha! Ha! Ha!'

His musical laugh sat oddly with the description, but the others seemed to find it equally amusing. I worried my grimace mightn't pass for a smile.

'If I 'ate anyone more than Leeds. Cants dan this.'

Tiger lifted his bomber jacket, revealing a long scar across his lower back. 'Seventy-three that were.'

'Wot? Stitches?'

'Nah. 1973.'

''Ow many then?'

'For'y.'

'So 'ow many you go' al'gether?'

Tiger started touching parts of his head and body, calculating to himself as he did so.

''Bout two 'undred an' eigh'ee. Wha' abah' you?'

'Trade secret, mate.'

'I've got two 'undred an' all.' Bill was proud.

'Abah' you, Denz?'

'Too many ter mention, man.'

A blonde girl started screaming further down the carriage.

'Cam on, love. Show's wha' you got under that scarf!'

A skinny bloke with dark, curly hair and little round glasses started to lift the hand-woven red and white scarf that fell across her breasts. She pushed him back and he allowed himself to fall across the table while his mate moved in behind and noisily pretended to bugger him, shaking a can of lager that climaxed with half its contents spurting over everyone in the vicinity. The first man ran his hand across the girl's tear- and lager-stained cheek. She brought her right hand up and cracked him hard across the face. I feared for her, but he just sat back in his seat, muttering loudly to himself, 'I ain't gonna 'it 'er, I ain't, 'cos if I did I'd put 'er cant's 'ead through the fackin' floor!'

As we whizzed through Watford Junction and the conversation turned to future fixtures, I began to wonder whether I had the ability to repeat my story in cold blood.

''Boro next week, innit?' asked Tiger for want of anything better to say. This was my chance.

'Yeah, but I won't be there.'

'Nah?'

'Won't be going for a while now.'

'Why's that? Goin' on 'oliday?'

Elly's response.

'Nah, inside.'

''Ow long for?'

'Dunno, four years.'

I trusted Elly would eventually fill them in on the details.

'I'll save the programmes for yer!'

I wondered how easy it would be to find such loyalty at Oxford.

The Oxford Classicist

Τι δε τισ; τι δ ου τισ; σκιασ ουαρ αυθρωποσ
(What is someone? What no one? Man is a shadow's
dream)

Pindar, Pythian Odes 8.95

*'Hey! Would you like to see them sitting together on the moun-
tain?'*

  'Of course! I'd give a fortune in gold for that.'
  'Why this sudden great curiosity?'
  'Well it'd be a shame to see them drunk, but . . .'
  'You'd enjoy their shame?'
  'But can I hide beneath the ash trees?'
  'If you're concealed they'll hunt you down.'
  'Alright, I won't hide. I take your point.'
  'But, if I agree to take you, will you come?'
  'Right away! I can't wait!'
  'First put this fine linen dress on.'
  'Why? Do I have to become a woman?'
  'If they see you're a man, they'll kill you.'
  'I'm not sure about "Hey!"'

My tutor's tone was wry, almost amused. We were sitting
side by side at his desk, uncomfortably close, and when I
turned to reply, he flicked his head away like a horse with
an irritating fly.

  'Ha!' Godfrey exclaimed forcefully.

I sat up abruptly. The full weight of his donnish stare was being brought to bear on my right temple. Now I was the one unable to hold eye contact.

'Ha!' he repeated, triumphantly. 'It's practically the same as the Greek *A!* This is where Dionysus really knows he has Pentheus.' His voice was well-modulated but flat, like an echo over water.

'Dodds suggests "Stop!" but I don't find that necessary. Otherwise you're basically accurate. How are you finding it?'

Behind the inquisitorial black-framed glasses, his blue eyes were filled with an almost parental concern.

'I think it's extraordinary.'

'Dionysus is a pretty extraordinary figure.'

We were facing each other across the ring again.

'Do you think Euripides was dealing with real events?' he feinted.

I wondered which way he was going. For a few seconds our heads flicked back and forth like the flippers on a pinball machine while I weighed his question.

'Well Pentheus was mythological,' I shifted, trying to achieve balance.

'I don't mean that.' His glasses had become menacing extensions of his eyes. 'At the time Euripides was writing the cult of Dionysus was alive and well in Athens.'

'But people weren't being torn apart by its celebrants.'

'Only in the myth, although there might have been the odd cow or two.'

'Surely Dionysus' destruction of Pentheus represents the triumph of the irrational over the rational.'

'Or the fear of that triumph.'

Again I felt the force of his gaze on my temple.

'I suppose being torn limb from limb by your own mother and sister is a fairly horrifying prospect' (the Cockney Reds were tame by comparison) 'but doesn't Euripides advocate the triumph of the irrational,

Divine power moves
Slowly but surely,
Correcting those who
In crazed perversity
Worship senseless folly
Not the godly

Which here refers, oxymoronically, to Dionysus?'

'Yah, but those are the words of the Bacchants, and not only that, they're in a trance! It's special pleading. I think you'd be hard-pushed to prove that was Euripides' own line.'

I'd hurtled across the ring only to be thrown to the floor by a more experienced opponent.

I felt certain that Euripides must come down on the side of the god Dionysus, whose orgiastic rituals and ecstatic way of life Pentheus is so desperate to destroy, chiefly because he cannot come to terms with his own animal urges.

Go swift hounds of Madness, go to the mountain
Where the daughters of Cadmus are joined in worship.
Whip them up against the mad spy, Pentheus . . .
Let Justice visible walk. Let Justice sworded walk,
Stabbing home to the throat
The godless, the lawless, the conscienceless one,
Earthborn of Echion the serpent's breed.

Then Godfrey changed tack, asking me how things were otherwise; I told him I could do with meeting more people. It was as close as I'd come to acknowledging my loneliness but he read the subtext. He tried to reassure me, suggesting that many of my peers had arrived from schools with strong Oxbridge traditions and probably already knew quite a few people. Perhaps I might find the answer in the Chapel Choir where I'd also be able to pursue my singing. Had I met the organ scholar? But before I could answer, he placed his hands on the desk and hoisted himself abruptly to his full six feet two, indicating that proceedings were finished. My 'Goodbye' was met by a right hand raised in a Roman 'Vale!' which was then slapped down on the desk.

* * *

The organ scholar's was the only acceptable room on my staircase, one of the town houses in Pembroke Street that had been converted to form the North Quad so that its front doors now opened onto undergraduate life and away from the sins of the world of the town beyond. My own cell could scarcely contain its essentials; the door would bang into the bed as I entered, just missing the 'comfy' chair en route, while my desk, facing the street, allowed me to lean over my texts and prod passers-by through the window if the mood so took me. I'd also experienced the Chapel Choir. There were three of us, all basses (the tenor was off playing croquet for the college) and none of us could sight-read. Although the organ scholar, a precise and demanding musician, was unable to suppress his irritation, membership of the Chapel Choir brought other benefits. The Chaplain invited me to pre-evensong drinks in Broadgate's Hall. Dandruff and bad breath were the order of the day, and I soon realised that most people there, myself included, used the drinks and nibbles as a form of defence, raising glasses to maintain a safe distance while ensuring that their mouths were filled briefly enough to allow for the niceties of polite conversation, but never long enough to engage in anything more. The Chaplain himself floated between the chompers and guzzlers in his long robes, smiling genially.

Such were the sight-singing capabilities of our three basses, that harmonies undreamed of by Stamford, or possibly even Stockhausen, broke the chill air of the eighteenth-century chapel. It was embarrassingly full, confirming my suspicion that the college's proportion of practising Christians exceeded the national average. I was Satan on my staircase, where everyone seemed to be recruiting for the Oxford Intercollegiate Christian Union. One, having glimpsed me at evensong, even turned up at my door with *Good News from John*.

'So, if you're Jewish, why are you singing in the Chapel Choir?'

I told him that the only place I'd ever refuse to sing would be on the Kippax with City, but that seemed to confuse him even more. I was sure they all met in the showers at night to discuss whether to try me by fire or water.

The loneliness chilled me, and the sound of revelry outside and doors opening and shutting to the accompaniment of salutations within accentuated its bitterness. To my shame I found myself phoning home nightly. Once again Dad dug out his own contacts, whose parties and dinners I enjoyed, but Italy had taught me that this was not the way forward, and that I needed to establish my own, independent circle.

Failure at the Blues football trials seemed to confirm Biti's verdict. Unable to shake off a niggling left-back, who surreptitiously tugged my shirt whenever he wasn't actually first to the ball, I was side-lined after twenty minutes, dreams of Wembley evaporated, though I had more success with the college team, in which I shared the right-wing spot. Newly promoted to the top division, and bolstered by two blues, we were confident of our chances in the university championship. At Pimlico, threats of 'I'm gettin' off this bus first or you'll get my fackin' fist dahn your throat!' from the captain, and a warning of 'If you turn up to trainin' we'll kick your fackin' bollocks off' from the rest of the squad, had convinced me that the school team probably wasn't for me. Consequently I'd developed my skills as a yard player during lunch-breaks, and now I found it difficult to adapt to the disciplined regime of the Pembroke first eleven. They relied on fitness and aggression rather than skill. Instead of receiving the ball to feet, I found myself eternally chasing upfield hoofs in a race with whichever left-back happened to be marking me. 'Hurt him, Mark! Hurt him! Hurt him! Hurt him!' yelled my captain who would one day find fame as brief to Nick Leeson. I was encouraged to collide with the opposition goalkeeper and to stud my marker at the earliest opportunity. Before long we had the worst disciplinary record in the league, and the sending-off of our stalwart scouse right-back for fighting was the straw that broke Harold Thompson's back. Chairman of the Football Association as well as the University's, he bestowed on us the distinction of being the first side ever to be expelled from the University league, and forbade any other college side to play us, even in a friendly, on pain of being banished themselves. We were top of the division at the time.

* * *

Options seemed to be running out fast as I walked into hall one evening, still without a regular table to sit at. I found the only available space at the front, just beneath High Table, within spitting distance of the Master had the mood taken him. The bearded bloke sitting opposite scrutinised my jacket.

'Is that a Rangers badge?'

'Yup.'

'Och! Doesn't miss those! You a fresher?'

'Aha.'

'What are you studying?'

'Classics.'

His eyes narrowed in curiosity.

'What's yer name?'

'Mark.'

'You're Brian Glanville's son!'

I confessed. His grey eyes twinkled below the sweep of dark hair that fell across his brow.

'Hey, Matt! Guess who this is! Ah've found him! It's Brian Glanville's son!'

The guy sitting next to me turned slowly, as if he meant to express the disinterest this news inspired in him. His thin blonde hair framed a nose that looked as if it had been broken in six places.

'So, do you have a name?' he asked in a measured Yorkshire accent.

'Mark,' I repeated.

His frown dissolved and he extended his hand.

'We all read your old man here, don't we, boys?'

There was a consensus of nodding heads. My attempts

at fielding their questions were silenced by the jaw-tingling scritch of heavy wooden benches being dragged across stone as the assembled undergraduate masses stood for grace. While the Latin words stumbled over the tongue of a dyslexic chemist I felt Matt's calves flex against the bench. It fell to the ground with a crash that echoed round the sepulchral hall. Pairs of donnish eyes peered menacingly through their spectacles in our direction. There was only one bench on the floor, so the source of the disturbance was obvious. My companions didn't even twitch and, as the grace climaxed, most of them joined in loudly with the final *alamur, foveamur, corroboremur* (may we be nourished, nurtured and strengthened). The Stretford End had met *Carmina Burana*.

'So, what's it like being the son of a famous father?'

A chirpy Liverpudlian with dark curly hair and vivacious blue eyes was staring at me challengingly.

'What's it like to be a Scouse?' I replied in the well-drilled patter of the Cockney Reds.

'Good Lord!' exclaimed Matt, swapping Yorkshire for Eton. 'Bit cocky for a fresher, what!'

'Now, now, chaps!' chimed in another, following suit.

'Yes, steady on there, men!'

'Yah! Steady on! Steady on!' chorused the table.

'Anyway, Mark,' said the Scotsman, with an enormous grin, 'what *is* it like being the son of a famous writer?'

'You bastards!' I smiled.

'You bawstards!' echoed the Scotsman, exaggerating my London accent.

'Bawstards, bawstards!' said the others.

'So have you met Godfrey yet?' asked the Scotsman.

'Ages ago. Good man.'

'He's a cunt!'

'Why?'

''Cos he's a fucking snob and a bad-tempered bawstard!'

'Hey Andy! You're getting in the young girl's way!' yelled the scouser.

'Och! Sorry, Maria.'

A pretty girl smiled sweetly and deposited a tureen of dark liquid on the table.

'Any bread, Maria . . . please?' asked Matt, now back in the dales.

'You 'ere again?' she asked in a soft local accent.

'Aye!' said Andy. 'You can't keep him away. The food in Worcester's even worse than here!'

The girl giggled.

'Maria! Have you met Mark?'

She nodded. I'd been served by her a few times on less boisterous tables. As I spooned the soup into my bowl, some of it spilt onto the table. Its watery texture traced an easy course to the edge and onto my white chinos.

'Honestly, Baba!' Maria exclaimed. 'I'll have to get you a cloth.'

'Honestly, Baba!' Andy laughed and the rest of the table followed suit.

By the time I was cleaned up, beef stew and anaemic boiled potatoes had arrived.

'Harry!' cried Matt, taking one of the potatoes, placing it in his spoon and catapulting it across the hall. It landed in a glass someone was raising to his lips. There was the satisfying sound of breaking glass. The victim looked inquiringly across, as if he expected our table to be the source of the crime, but caught no one's eye.

At the end of the meal I was asked whether I fancied going to the Junior Common Room for a game of bar-footie. This was home territory, as we had a table in Holland Park where I regularly thrashed Dad, and even had written records to prove it. The common room was located in the oldest part of the college, but behind the elegant yellow-stone façade was a coffee-stained carpet, tattered walls and battered furniture strewn with over-thumbed newspapers. It was split-level, the top part consisting of a sort of games room where tall figures in flowing scholars' gowns bent over a pool table, studiously manipulating the cues. Commoners' gowns, comprised of a central strip and two limp wings, flapped ludicrously at the bar-footie table, arms jerking frantically with the effort of knocking a small plastic ball into the opposing goal. Matt put six ten-pence pieces down as deposit, effectively monopolising the table. When his turn came he was joined by Andy and the two of them annihilated the opposing pair in minutes. After an hour of pub games we retired to the TV room, where Matt and Harry turned to News at Ten on ITV despite the protests of someone watching a documentary on Cambodia. But it wasn't the news that interested them. They were competing to be the first to spot the brand being advertised at the start of each commercial. Not a game I'd win.

'Not going yet, Mark?' said Matt.

'Essay to finish.'

'Och! Godfrey can wait!'

'Nah. If he's got an essay to do let 'im go,' said Harry.

'Jus' 'cos you're a fucking swot!' joked Andy. 'Nay mind! We'll see yer tomorrow. Goodnight Baba!'

'You bastards!' I grinned.

'You bawstards!' they all repeated.

I wanted space to savour that evening's rare sensation of belonging, and rather than risk going to the showers, and bumping into one of the Christians who might diminish it, I returned to my room, pissed in the sink and went to bed.

I ran into Andy the following day at the pigeonholes. He invited me to a Tamla and Soul evening in the Long Room at New College which he assured me all the lads would be attending.

* * *

'I've loved this man ever since I was a kid! There's no one like him!'

On came *Rockin' Robin*. Tarantini, the disc-jockey, hair as fuzzy as the footballer's after whom he was nicknamed, emerged from behind the turntable in his white T-shirt and red braces to join the hoofing throng. Matt stood aside, downing a bottle of lager and assessing the situation. I went over to have a chat with him.

'You see those guys over there?'

He pointed out a small group of punks in leather jackets who were pogoing inappropriately by the DJ area, periodically hitting the wooden trestle table supporting the turntable, bouncing the stylus over the vinyl as they did so. The lads couldn't possibly keep their rhythm in the face of such distraction, and Tarantini's priceless collection was being damaged to boot.

'Townies?'

Matt lowered his head and raised it again with a flick,

signalling to me to follow him. Most of the dancers were too engrossed to detect any shift in atmosphere, but Matt's Worcester friends were alerted. A couple of punks started to eye us. Matt shoved against one of them.

'What's your problem, mate?' he asked in an ugly, Cowley burr. Encouraged by the presence of a number of Matt's firm, I moved in front of the punk.

'You are!' I said.

I took in his Mohican, the feather earring, his cheap leather jacket embellished with the names of mainstream punk bands. Only playing at it, I thought. His mates assembled behind him and a space cleared.

'You're not welcome here,' warned Matt, his face and voice utterly expressionless, a parody of Clint Eastwood. The punk caught him hard in the jaw with a swift right uppercut. Matt didn't flinch, nor did he retaliate. This fazed his opponent. The aggressive triumph that had flushed his face as the blow landed drained away, but the expected mayhem never occurred, and the other punks followed their leader who clearly thought better of it, past us towards the exit. I looked at Matt. His eyes were radiant.

'Come on!' he ordered in a guttural voice, and turned away from me, exhorting his firm, fixing each of them in turn. He looked almost insane.

Without looking back, Matt left the Long Room and moved rapidly down the steps. I wasn't as sure as him. I turned my head and only registered four others leaving the disco. We were outnumbered. As we approached the passageway between the two quads I could hear yelling and shouting ahead, but, emerging at the other end, I was relieved to see them racing for the porter's lodge on Holywell Street, terrorising the people they met. As yet they hadn't noticed us. Matt had us moving at a brisk pace but still walking, keeping our cool while, I hoped, the punks were losing theirs.

By the time we reached the porter's lodge Matt had almost broken into a trot and the five of us were huddled behind him. As we entered Holywell Street, the punks were nowhere to be seen. Matt looked left and right, lifting his head as if to inhale their odour, swung confidently to the right and started to run. Although I hoped he'd got it wrong, it was more likely they'd be heading for the High Street than the heart of the University. And, at that moment, that's exactly where I wanted to be; a student surrounded by lots of other students. This felt more like a night match with the Cockney Reds in Leeds.

Matt was right. About fifty yards ahead I made out a cluster of Mohicans and shaved heads. Matt had a grievance, but I couldn't get worked up about it. Tonight there were no badges or scarves, and I was afraid.

Holywell Street was empty. Before turning into Longwall Street we took time to compose ourselves, so when we appeared we'd look confident and organised, too much for this gaggle of ramshackle punks.

'Look!' cried Harry. 'I think one of 'em's got a blade!'
    Matt picked up a broken brick. Someone else smashed a bottle and held its serrated remains against the light of a street lamp. Harry handed me a bottle, which I clenched tightly to my side, more like a comfort toy than a weapon. This was getting serious. I'd never used a tool and had

never intended to. The punks carried on towards the High Street, glanced back at us, and disappeared round the corner. As Matt reached the end of Longwall Street he let out a raucous cry, and rounded the corner in one huge bound. I followed him quickly. To my horror the punks were ranged against us with knives, bottles, bricks and a scaffolding pole nicked from a building site. It was either fight or run and, as my legs had turned to jelly, I had to stand.

'Come on, you cunts! Let's 'ave yer!' yelled their leader, but as they charged and we stood our ground a police van loomed into view. Everyone dropped their weapons and ran. The muscles in my legs recovered. This was a different kind of fear. No one would blame me for escaping arrest. I was off with Matt and the rest of the crew, back up Longwall Street. The police spilled out of the van in pursuit of the fleeing punks. No one seemed to follow us down Longwall Street, but we thought it best to put as much distance as possible between ourselves and the situation.

We carried on up Holywell Street, retracing our steps, past New College and down to the King's Arms.

'Fancy a pint, Mark?'

'Normal night for you, Matt?'

'Lord no!' he replied in his fake Etonian accent. 'Old nerves couldn't take it, what? Get that pint dahn yer! Harry! Right, we're off. Things to do!'

I was still buzzing when I got back to Pembroke, so I went to the JCR and found Andy bent over the bar-footie table as I'd expected. I called out to him.

'Who's that?'

'Mark.'

'Och, Baba! How're ye keeping? I'm just . . . showing . . . AJ . . . how to . . .' Kerploch! The plastic ball hammered into the back of the wooden goal. 'Oh shite!'

'Tough luck, Andy!' his stocky Indian adversary commiserated, adjusting a skin-tight leather glove to which he applied some talc. A small can of oil watched over his goal.

'Baba, do yer fancy a game? You'll have to play AJ. He's just beaten me again, the bawstard!' he grinned.

I was out of my depth. When I finally pulled one back at o–4 down he twitched in irritation, adjusted his glove and applied some oil to his full-backs, as if castigating them for being too slow.

'Fuckin' 'ell! The bar-footie Olympics!'

'AJ doesn't get out very often, Baba.'

Kerplock! AJ's face eased as the winning goal went in. He lifted the top of the table to retrieve the balls for his next victim. There were no takers.

Andy took us back to his room, which was decorated with the black and amber scarves and pennants of his beloved East Fife Football Club. He poured us each half a pint of Scotch while I recounted the night's events, wondering to myself whether he was sorry to have missed them.

'Matt's a great guy, but I try to keep out of the way when he gets like that.'

'The thing I like about Matt is he's salt of the earth, working class.'

Andy and AJ exchanged surprised looks.

'What makes you think Matt's working class?'

Oundle-educated, son of an MP, brother to a top academic, athletics blue; Matt had taken me in as surely as I had Elly.

Oxford's very short, eight-week terms meant that a three-year course was completed in half that time, and life was conducted at a commensurate speed and intensity. Brief friendships appeared lifelong and relationships burned with the intensity of a holiday romance. Such an existence was conducive to all the recklessness of a 'here today, gone tomorrow' Epicureanism without the philosophy. Two weeks of lawlessness followed during which bicycles were stolen to order with the aid of a fast hacksaw blade I'd acquired to break the lock on my own bike; television sets were half-inched from JCRs; the contents of drinks cabinets from SCRs; more townie gangs confronted, right-wing students targeted. Most of our activities were rationalised, somewhat dubiously, as attacks on the establishment. One speciality was emptying fruit machines and games tables for their profits. There was talk of hiring a van, going to Cambridge dressed in workmen's overalls, and systematically going round each college, breaking into their machines under the guise of repairing them.

It was hardly the Oxford of *Brideshead Revisited* (if anything my new milieu was closer to Tiger's than Sebastian Flyte's and this unexpected familiarity undoubtedly eased my acclimatisation), but I felt that I was at last being accepted for what I was. There was wonderfully little uniformity, plenty of eccentricity, and an exciting fizz that gave most people a shock and saw them react in different ways. On the face of it Oxford seemed to tip its cap to Church and State, but with backs turned it was cocking a snook. It could be no other way in a town where sceptics laboured through the night to unpick religious and ethical systems that had audaciously dressed their relative morality in *a priori* livery. Where no law was easily justified lawlessness could flourish, even if it wasn't polite to say so.

* * *

Coming home, I was particularly aware of how much I'd changed, but I was also confronted by the reality of where I'd so recently come from. One afternoon, chatting with Mum, I realised I'd missed the first five minutes of an old Tito Gobbi film. The TV was on. Toby was lolling on the sofa, and barely reacted as I came in.

'Nice to see your brother again?'

'Don't flatter yourself.'

'Tobe, can we turn over? There's an opera I'd like to see on the other side.'

His jet-black eyes focused coldly on the screen, looking rather than watching.

'Tobe, you're not really interested in this. Please!'

'Why don't you go back to Oxford and all your pimply friends?'

I stood in front of him and pulled a couple of stupid faces. He didn't react, so I snatched the remote control from his hands, smiled sarcastically, and changed channels to Tito Gobbi.

'Fucking put it back!'

'Get stuffed!'

'I'm warning you!'

'You've got a fucking nerve, you little cunt! I come back home, I haven't seen you for two months, you can't even be fucking bothered to say hello, now you want to fuck up my programme!'

'Don't call me a cunt!'

'You are. You're a little cunt!'

He slid off the couch and drew himself to his full height. He wasn't little anymore. Charging at me menacingly he tried to grab the control. We ended in a bundle on the sofa. Powerful punches smashed into my spine and kidneys. I couldn't find the space to swing and hit him back, but as he delivered a right cross that missed and slammed into the wall, I caught him in the solar plexus. My head was smashed repeatedly against the wall.

'Hey! Hey! Hey!'

In stormed Dad, made a B-line for me, and shoved me roughly into the corner of the sofa, wrenching the skin on my shoulder. It felt as if nothing had changed in seventeen years: Toby crying wolf, Dad protecting him, and something inside me collapsed. 'What's the matter? I didn't hurt you?'

'You always do!'

The anguish hurt more than the blows.

'You love Toby more than me. You always did. You always will!'

I wept like the child I felt reduced to. Dad let out a sigh of exasperation.

'Pa-am!' he yelled. 'For fuck's sake get up here! They're fighting again. Cain and Abel!'

I fled to my room and looked for Tony Pawson's *Official History of the F.A. Cup*. Dad and I had attended its launch. It was a special, boxed edition, and down its spine was a long, stiletto-like paper knife engraved with a picture of the F.A. Cup. I rolled back my sleeve and dragged it repeatedly across the back of my left wrist.

* * *

''Ey, Baba. Wharr'appened to yer arm?'

'Cat.'

Harry smiled disbelievingly.

'Are you sure you didn't do it yourself?'

'Big fucking cat.'

'I do it sometimes yer know. Gerr' a blade an' slice meself op a bit.'

'Why?'

'Oh, I dunno. 'Ard ter explain, really. Why do you do it?'

'Better I do it to myself, not someone else.'

'Aye, that's it.'

He told me Matt had hurt himself badly after the New College confrontation by smashing up a mirror in the King's Arms. I hazarded a guess that the mirror hadn't come off too well either.

'Fock the mirror, pal! Jos' stops all those pooftahs lookin' at 'emselves!'

It was hard to imagine he was one of the college's brightest academic hopes.

* * *

Each Spring term, Oxford University Opera Club put on a production. This year it was *Fidelio*. I joined the chorus but the director drummed me out of the regiment for being unable to perform rifle drill, the one thing, as a former officer of the Black Watch, he was qualified to direct.

'You, sir, are removed from duty!'

I was forced to sit and watch as the looming, wire-wool haired figure gesticulated with twiglet arms in an attempt to mould his undergraduate corps into an elite garrison. Harder still was transforming a well-nourished bunch of young men into starving prisoners at the point of death.

We were informed excitedly by the conductor Denis Arnold, Oxford's Professor of Music, that the soloists would be coming from Glyndebourne. Hearing opera singers at close quarters in rehearsal made up for the frustration of not being able to sing much myself. Mark Raphael had never done much on the opera stage, his voice and persona being better suited to recitals and I was astonished by the sheer size and quality of sound some of the singers produced, like a magic trick.

There was a gauze curtain at the front of the stage, which the director sold to us as if it were the first vacuum cleaner, but I suspected he'd put it there to befuddle the audience, in the hope that by watching the action through a haze they might be less alert to its myriad shortcomings. In the final scene the heroine Leonore, in the male disguise that has allowed her to infiltrate the prison, wrests the knife from Pizarro's hand just as he is about to cut her lover's throat. As I came out on the first night to sing the final chorus celebrating the triumph of the forces of goodness and light, besides the gauzes and schmauzes and backdrops and schmackdrops that had appeared over the last twenty-four hours, I noticed little piles of blood that seemed to have been placed strategically at points about the stage. They looked just like the ones I'd deposited on the concourse at Pimlico all those years ago when Les broke my nose. If this was the director's macabre final gesture, I wasn't impressed. Not until we left the stage to luke-warm applause did I realise why the blood was so convincing. Stage staff had failed to blunt the razor-sharp, genuine Bowie knife wielded by Pizzarro, and poor Leonore had sliced through her hand. Ambulance men were attending her as we left the stage, and she was forced to perform the remainder of the run in a rather anachronistic Boots bandage. For once Pizarro had got a result, reality breaking through to realise the evil intentions of art with the help of a dodgy props girl.

Other members of the back-stage crew laboured hard and long to turn pink-cheeked students into shit-stained convicts. One such was Chrissie, always cheerful and friendly, long, hennaed hair switching like a horse's mane across the back of her T-shirt. She plastered on the slap more enthusiastically than her colleagues, determined to uglify even the freshest-faced Adonises. With me it was a losing battle. Vanity got the better of dramatic intention, and each evening I'd return to my dressing-room and smear her handiwork until I could see myself again. Other make-up artists might have been less exacting, but I was happy to spend time destroying her artwork in exchange for a little flirtation, not something found easily at Oxford. Women were still greatly outnumbered by men. As a result many came over as stand-offish or even arrogant. No doubt they were fed up with unwanted male attention, but some seemed fooled by the unreality of the situation into believing they really were the latest incarnation of Sophia Loren.

We came to the final performance with no more injuries to report besides those inflicted on the opera.

'We've been told to make you look really horrible tonight,'

beamed Chrissie. 'The director thinks you look too much like a bunch of students.'

'Funny that!'

He was right. It was more like a health farm than a prison. I looked in the mirror. She'd transformed me into a filthy old convict, just the sort of character who might lunge and grab her round the waist while she'd obligingly scream.

'You know, you're really good at this,' I flattered, feeling the firm curve of her waist sift through my hands. 'I look at myself, I can't sleep nights.'

She laughed. Wiping away her hard work as usual, tonight I added a little extra to my costume. Dad was coming. I thought he'd appreciate the black, red and white scarf I wrapped round my shin, hoping it might pass for a bandage. He was the only one to notice.

'You absolute imbecile!'

Had they enjoyed it?

'Ghastly production. Dreadful, screeching soprano.'

Mum hadn't.

'And some lousy Stretford Ender hobbling about in a United scarf!'

'Scoreboard Paddock!' I corrected him.

I prayed Chrissie would be at the cast party. I found her chatting with another member of the chorus, glass of wine in hand, laughing and smiling. I grabbed a glass, took a couple of swigs and approached them.

'Hi!'

'Hi!' she smiled enthusiastically. My rival raised his glass to his lips protectively.

'Well, I thought we were all looking pretty goddamned ugly tonight! I hope you're proud of yourself.'

As she giggled, I remembered one of Dad's *mots*: 'If you can make a woman laugh, you're halfway into bed with her.' The other bloke smiled nervously and wandered off. I started telling her about my operatic aspirations and she seemed genuinely interested.

'I love the theatre, but I can't really do anything myself.'

'Have you tried?'

'It's embarrassing, really!' She gave an earthy chuckle. By now I'd normally have tripped over my own penis, but arousal was fuelling my every word, look and movement, so I asked her back for coffee at Pembroke, just a couple of minutes' walk away.

Back in my cell, I switched on the kettle, spooned out the Nescafe, and sat beside her on the bed. The very lack of furniture facilitated seduction. I looked into her eyes. They were receptive and at ease and, as I leant forward to kiss her, I knew she wouldn't rebuff me. Within seconds we were lying across the bed, fumbling and caressing.

'Let's take our clothes off.'

It felt so forward, but each button on her blouse, the zip on her jeans, were hurdles at which I might fall. I couldn't have borne to be so close and let that happen. To my joy Chrissie smiled, stood up, and followed my suggestion. I watched as her body was unveiled. Someone I barely knew until that evening was naked right in front of me. I loved her naturalness and lack of shame. Before you could say *Namenloser Freude*, we were making love.

'Do you do this a lot? I bet you've got dozens of girl friends!'

I couldn't admit she was the first girl I'd slept with since coming to Oxford, and only the second girl ever.

'Why didn't you come?'

My puffing and groaning hadn't fooled her.

'It doesn't matter. I just wanted you to enjoy it.'

'I did. But I'd enjoy it even more if you did.'

Chrissie smiled at me with such affection I felt sad. Some unknown guilt was blocking the ecstatic, Bacchic release I craved. But I'd found my Dionysus.

* * *

We met again the following weekend. Chrissie turned up at Pembroke drenched in Diorella. What with the sensation of her hand moving over my body, the firm curvaceousness of her own, and eyes that bored through to my groin as swiftly as her perfume had, our plans for the evening were scuppered.

'Let's get between the sheets.'

Last time we'd stayed there until the evening of the following day. She admitted she had a boyfriend but it was coming to an end, and as long as we remained in bed I felt she was mine. Sex was part of an overall sensation of warmth and security, but, much though I enjoyed it, its climax continued to remain elusive.

Besides sex, Chrissie offered a refreshingly un-Oxford normality. Her small studio flat was in the tree-lined north of the city. Like so many other rooms I knew at that time it was dominated, literally and figuratively, by its bed, a double mattress with a psychedelic spread to which everything gravitated. Chrissie's clothes and belongings were draped over backs of chairs and down walls in a relaxed, easy fashion. She'd break tiny flakes of dope off a shit-brown block and roll nicotine-heavy joints we'd smoke to relax even more, although when we kissed her little cats would jump on my back and claw me through my shirt.

'They're stoned,' she giggled. 'They always do that.'

I wondered how many others they'd marked. Was she still seeing Mike, her old boyfriend? I asked her with feigned unconcern.

'Oh no. We're still friends, that's all.'

In the morning we'd lean out of the window looking onto the overgrown garden and sometimes greet people walking past. Peaceful and filled with birdsong, it seemed much more than a mile from the city centre.

We went down to my parents' house in Dorset for a long weekend and cycled round the lanes where bright new blossom glistened and dew released the fresh aroma of spring. In the evenings we made a log fire and smoked ourselves like kippers before the nest-blocked chimney whilst finishing off bottles of Martini and lemonade, and reading MR James ghost stories – standard family activities I was happy to share with Chrissie. In the near distance was a little copse where I'd once or twice seen deer, and in front of it a glade in which rabbits played. Sometimes you'd see a hare. It was where I'd go to lose myself when I needed to escape the family, and to bring someone else there was like revealing my sacred spot. I barely noticed the gradual disintegration of the wood and mud that had so long blocked the channel of my libido, but in the end the dam broke below. I felt vulnerable, as though I'd confided a secret I'd always been afraid to reveal, and then, too soon, we had to leave. Like a child with a new toy I was desperate to re-experience the new sensation at every opportunity, even up to the very point when the cab driver arrived to take us to the station, twenty minutes early of course, and had to wait in his car while we unravelled the spaghetti of knickers and jeans.

I felt Chrissie wasn't aware of its significance to me or how it had altered the balance of our relationship. Now she was very much more important to me I wanted to be with her all the time, yet the deeper my feelings became the more frivolous she was. I saw potential rivals everywhere, in pubs, where she always seemed to know some carefree individual, and at discos and parties where I'd constantly want her in view. I realised that my behaviour was driving her away but I couldn't stop myself.

'I didn't know you, did I? I thought you were just after a good time, not like this, on my case the whole time. It's driving me mad.'

* * *

Luckily, *Mother Courage* distracted me. Sean, one of the few non-Christians on my staircase, a pallid, orange-haired individual, always in black, had heard me warbling in the urinals and offered me a part in his upcoming production. It may have been his way of circumventing possible objections, since he planned to perform the play on the paved area directly in front of our staircase, a ready-made stage where the pond formed an orchestra pit. I was to kick off, singing 'Here's Mother Courage and her wagon' in the specially created role of Prologue. But my loyalties were split. There was opposition from my friends at Table Six.

'What's that fockin' arty prick thinkin'? There's people'll

be revisin' fer their Finals while that fockin' racket's goin' on. 'E can' gerr' away with it!'

And once the dons had okayed the production, sabotage was the topic of the day. It felt odd to be privy to plotting and scheming aimed at wrecking the play I was actually in. One seriously discussed plan was for someone in a wetsuit to secrete himself in the murky waters of the pond and emerge half way through the evening to steal everyone's thunder. I wondered if that wouldn't simply end up being construed as a bit of Brechtian alienation, like the daily changing colour of the pond the same chap had effected, much to the amusement of the cast.

Smoke signals were sent to Worcester, and Matt arrived for a pow-wow. To the side of the stage lay a gardener's hose that might be used to drench performers and audience alike on the final night. As I went out for the last time as Prologue and scene announcer I saw the lads in position and was glad that I'd thwarted them. Earlier in the day I'd sliced through the hose in six places with my flick-knife.

Chrissie came to the cast party. She'd enjoyed the show, but not me.

'You didn't have any energy. Everyone else looked as if they were having a great time. Each time you came on it was like a vacuum.'

Rather than hear any more, I kept my distance from her, spending the evening with one of the stagehands, a student at St Hilda's who kept resting her hand on my thigh. I told Chrissie later, thinking I'd win brownie points for being faithful.

'You should've gone with her. I believe in that sort of thing.'

Next day I found out that Harry had broken into Sean's room where the run's entire proceeds were stashed but had been unable to find them.

'Looked fockin' everywhere. Bastards!'

'I can't believe it. Someone's ransacked my room!' Sean told me later. 'Do you think they might have been looking for the takings?'

* * *

Chrissie found herself a job working in 'The Bear', an ostensibly charming medieval pub. Situated behind Christ Church and in sight of Oriel, its location made it a haven for the rugby and rowing hearties attached to those predominantly public school colleges – and the kind of place I would normally have stayed well clear of.

'Come on, darling! Does it take as long to pull you as it does to pull that pint?' joked some beefcake in a rugby shirt. I tried to burn a hole through his hooped torso with my eyes, but he turned and smiled as if he expected to see a friend, so I glared directly at him. He was oblivious, but Chrissie wasn't. She scowled at me before turning to serve the next heartie who was ogling her. I began to wonder why I'd come to the pub.

'You bonked her too?'

'Great pair of lungs!'

'House man, isn't he?'

'Fancy that barmaid with the tight little bum!'

Bubbles of conversation floated up and popped in the

dense atmosphere of the small low-ceilinged room as the pub's ancient door opened and shut, signalling the exits and entrances of sports-shirted frames, often complemented by smiling, Sloane sylphs in light blue shirts, neck-scarves and jeans. There was an overbearing, unquestioning self-confidence in speech and demeanour I found intolerable; indifference to the feelings of anyone who wasn't one of them.

A particularly enormous, curly-haired burly in an Oriel hockey shirt headed for the bar, shouldering aside his ilk like a prop forward. They didn't mind. The bar was a training ground, complete with scrums, rucks and lineouts as jars of ale were passed over customers' heads like rugby balls in a seething *perpetuum mobile*.

'Hello, Chrissie!'
   He knew her name.
   'Working hard tonight?'
   She smiled her lovely, open smile, pouting upper lip, perfect white teeth, green eyes brimming with sex. He leant on the bar.
   'You know you're the only one for me.'
   'Bet you say that to all the girls!'
   'There aren't any others.'
   'Liar!'
   As loverboy left the bar with his two foaming pots I shouldered into him, Jewish, state-school, football-style. He looked down at his ale-sodden hands, then up and into my eyes. This wasn't the game. I glared into his laser-blue stare. It was only friends in here. Who was I? I watched the cogitation. Had he flattened me on a rugby pitch? Cracked my shin with

a hockey stick? He glanced at his hands again, back at me, then moved on into the scrimmage. I felt someone looking at me and swung round. Chrissie threw me a furious look. I shrugged my shoulders, mimed a telephone call, barged my way through the training ground and out.

'What the hell did you think you were doing?'

'What do you mean?'

'You deliberately barged into that bloke.'

'I wanted to smack him one. Anyway, why are you defending him? Are you having an affair or something?'

'That's my business.'

'Are you?'

'Of course I'm not. Do you think I'd go with a guy like that?'

And I knew she wouldn't. The danger was more likely to come from someone like the man in the sailor shirt, the necktie and the earring who'd greeted her so knowingly one night in the Corn Dolly.

'Can I come over and talk to you?'

'It's late.'

'I know, but I need to.'

'Call me tomorrow.'

'Chrissie, please!'

'I'll call you tomorrow.'

I wasn't sure she would and I didn't wait to find out. It was teeming down. Every millimetre of my clothing was soaking and mud kicked up onto my trousers as I cycled up the Banbury Road, the noise and feel of the rain heightening my drama. By the time I arrived at her flat I had become the tragic hero of a Hardy novel, enamoured as never before.

I knocked gently and saw a light go on. The door was opened on a chain.

'What the hell are you doing here?'

I'd forgotten. While I had been riding with the Valkyries she had been asleep.

'Look at the state of you! You'd better come in.'

I took off my shirt and trousers and Chrissie gave me a towel to dry my hair.

'You can't stay. I've got to get up early tomorrow.'

'I just wanted to talk.'

'I told you I'd call you.'

'I know.'

My sodden state just irritated her. It was only a matter of time before I was out. We sat at opposite ends of her bed.

'You're always watching me, not trusting me.'

'Have you ever slept with anyone since we've been together?'

She didn't answer.

'You have?'

'It's none of your business.'

'Of course it is. You're my girlfriend.'

'I'm not yours. I'm not anybody's.'

'So who've you slept with?'

'Mike.'

She'd been two-timing me with her ex.

'When did you?'

'When I first started going out with you. I thought you knew that. We were together a long time, Mark.'

'How many times?'

'I don't know. Look. What's the point talking about it now? It's over.'

It was like a punch in my solar plexus. Over for whom? Me, Mike, or both of us? I panicked. Chrissie had become the cornerstone of the fragile structure I'd created for survival. If it collapsed, it would send me hurtling through its floorboards back to the basement I'd come from. Nothing would work without her. All the other parts of my life depended on her. I began to cry. She moved across the bed and put her arm around me.

'Don't cry.'

So she did have some sympathy left. I cried even more. She kissed the back of my head and stroked my damp cheek.

'Look, you can stay here tonight, if you want. Your clothes'll be dry by tomorrow.'

She pulled back the bedclothes. I climbed in next to her and clung to her like a child to a toy. She didn't respond, and that was how we fell asleep. When I woke, light was forcing its way through the cracks in the curtains. She'd gone.

I'd hoped she'd come with me to the latest Tamla/Soul disco Tarantini was holding in the Long Room. Her acute lateness had recently become chronic. But when she hadn't turned up after an hour and a half I decided it was terminal. I thought about staying in my room or even just putting the lights out and going to bed. Even if I just stayed in college Pembroke JCR was as uninspiring as ever, bar-footie and pool players bent down, peering over sticks at balls through curtains of greasy hair in the half-light.

When I got to New College, they were all there. Harry, Andy, and the Tamla crew in Daks and loafers, spinning and shuffling on leather soles to Marvin Gaye, plucking their imaginary braces to 'The Liquidator'.

'What's happenin', Mark?'

Matt was sizing up the dancefloor as he swigged a bottle of lager. 'You're not looking yourself.'

'Not feeling it.'

'Woman trouble?'

'Chrissie's stood me up. I reckon it's over.'

'Never mind. Get a beer down yer neck! What d'yer reckon to the disco?'

'Fab, but I'm not in the mood.'

'Nah, the gear.'

'Sounds great.'

'Top of the range. Hi-fi shop in Headington.'

'How come?'

He tapped the side of his nose with a forefinger.

'Fencing as well as athletics?'

'Come with me.'

I followed him out of the disco, down to an adjacent passageway where a flight of stone steps led to a cellar.

'Wait here and let me know if anyone comes.'

A minute later he was back.

'They're keeping all the Commem Ball champagne there. You up for it?'

As most of the revellers left, it slowly dawned on me that the gaggle remaining were all involved and I began to feel like Mia Farrow in *Rosemary's Baby*. There was Harry, of course, and a few faces I recognised from the night we'd confronted the punks. With nods and glances they dispersed to the rhythm of *Double Barrel*, another skinhead favourite from 1971 that sent images of my early days at Pimlico flashing through my head: for a moment I lost courage.

'Harry's gonna get his car and meet us outside the porter's lodge.'

It was too late to back out now.

It was one in the morning. The moon cast a beam like a helicopter searchlight across the immaculate lawn behind the Long Room. Matt returned to the cellar and I kept watch.

'Shit!'

'What is it?'

'Someone's locked the fookin' door!'

Which meant that someone also knew it had been opened. For a moment I hoped this would make Matt abandon the whole plan, but he responded with karate kicks. Anyone in the vicinity would have heard the tearing and cracking of splintering wood.

'Mark!'

He'd broken the two central panels, leaving enough room to climb through. Four huge sports holdalls materialised from nowhere. Adrenaline had mastered my fear, and I felt I could easily fend away the curious but no one came. Clinking and clanking like Marley's ghost, Matt climbed the steps, deposited two bags, and vanished again. Were anyone to walk past now I might find matters a little harder to explain. It felt like an age before he reappeared. I was shivering; my clothes, damp from dancing, growing icy in the cold night air.

'What took so long?'

'Boxes.'

'Boxes?'

'It's not all stored in neat little wine-racks, you know. I had to bag the cardboard. Bit of a giveaway!'

'So what's happening to it?'

'Mate of mine 'ere'll collect it. Right. Quiet as you can.'

We slunk through the narrow, cobbled alleyways, stopping in staircase entrances to avoid imaginary nightwalkers, sluggish with the immense weight we carried. We could hear voices, and New College's front quad offered no cover. At any moment someone might pass through the lodge and catch us on our final stretch. It was a risk, but we had no choice. In the hard light cast by the moon the sloping lawn and its surrounding gardens seemed as unreal as everything else, a virtual setting for virtual crime, and then, finally, we were at the porter's lodge. No one witnessed us. The porter was asleep at his desk.

'Where the fook's Harry?'

A car turned into Holywell Street and stopped outside the college. Inside a couple kissed passionately, unmindful of anything beyond their embrace. I thought about Chrissie. Under other circumstances I might have been tucked up in bed with her, fuelled by her warmth. The couple's passion seemed indulgent. Wouldn't it have been better catered to in a bedroom? And, in any case, as long as they remained there, our operation was in danger. Harry's white Fiesta pulled round the corner. Matt winked at me. Harry stopped and waited until the car in front drove away, having deposited, I hoped, a frustrated young man. We loaded the bags and drove off. A few minutes later we were at the back of New College.

'Come with me!'

Matt sprinted fifty yards and whistled. A window opened and a number of plastic bags were thrown out for us to catch, their handles neatly tied.

'The boxes,' Matt grinned.

Harry drove off and stopped on Hythe Bridge Street where we chucked the bags into the Cherwell.

'Fuckin' 'ell, Matt! This is clinical!'

He gave me a pitying look.

'Right, Harry. Drop us here.'

We were about a hundred yards from Worcester College lodge. I feared a reverse of our escape from New College, but Matt produced a key and unlocked a door on Worcester Street that led straight into the college's magnificent gardens, at which point we encountered a group of hippies playing frisbee.

'Fucking tossers! I've always hated hippies!'

'Don't knock 'em, Mark. Some of me best clients.'

He drew a deep drag on an imaginary spliff.

'What the fuck aren't you involved in, Matt?'

'Tell me what you want, I'll get it for yer.'

'Anything?'

'Blow, smack.'

It was a full hour before the moonlit frisbee came to an end and we clanked the final yards to Matt's room.

'Where the fuck's it all going?'

Matt dragged his bed aside and lifted the floorboards. I was surprised by the depth and space of the cavity beneath.

'Arthur Daley eat your heart out!'

I saw what I'd just risked my future for, as out came bottle after bottle of vintage champagne.

'Bollocks!'

'What's up?'

'These fooking labels!'

Each one bore New College's three rose motif and the inscription 1379–1979.

'I had a fence set up for this stuff. Now we'll have to fookin' drink it.'

I wondered how much I'd have seen for my efforts anyway, and reckoned that was the best possible thing to do.

Whether Chrissie was intrigued by what I'd done or just keen on free vintage champagne I wasn't sure, but our relationship enjoyed a brief renaissance that died a natural death with the long Summer vacation. It had really ended the night I cycled over in the pouring rain. But by rekindling the embers and then extinguishing them again, I could kid myself that she hadn't chucked me. To what must have been her most intense irritation I wrote her a letter outlining the reasons I felt our relationship could no longer work. We both knew the truth.

I lost the ballot for rooms that would have allowed me to remain in college. Staying would have been easier and I would have been upgraded, but the college walls served to imprison as well as protect. The bell in Christ Church's Tom Tower still struck ninety-nine times every evening at nine o'clock, each chime reminding a scholar to return to mater. We'd had to time the interval of *Mother Courage* to accommodate it, and although its significance was now largely symbolic, the university had not yet escaped the stranglehold of its monastic origins. Lovelorn Romeos still clambered over college walls, occasionally impaling themselves on spikes, risking rustication and castration in pursuit of their Juliets. But it suited some, among them, strangely, the Table-Six Crew, angry adolescents who resented and abused the over-zealous mother that nurtured them. Oxford was a convenient extension of the public school regimen I now knew they'd all grown up under.

*   *   *

Back in London I joined an employment agency called 'Problem'. I was put on the lowest rate of £1.50 an hour, and offered a job leafleting for an English language school that had reopened under a different name after going bust under highly dubious circumstances. My leafleting colleague, Edwin, a vivacious Geordie with wild blue eyes, would throw his boxes onto a skip as soon as the boss's back was turned.

'Right, I'm off to Lewisham for a meeting on Nicaragua. We're raising money for the Sandinistas.'

Despite his Tyneside origins he spoke with an almost camp, south-east feyness and I wasn't surprised to learn he was one of the many out of work actors the agency employed. Next day it was a conference on undermining the right-wing regime in Chile and the day after that he brought his girlfriend along.

'I reckon we can shift a lot more of these boxes if there's three of us.'

And now Amanda also earned £12 a day for attending left-wing conferences, or drinking coffee in Hyde Park. In the end I joined them.

'I don't feel guilty. Why should I? That bastard's ripping off all those people. He's just a fucking capitalist. It's our duty to steal from him,' but, as we lay on the grass tanning ourselves, his justifications seemed as lame as the ones we concocted to explain away our crimes at Oxford.

'Your surname's Glanville, isn't it? You're not by any chance related to Brian Glanville?'

I admitted I was.

'You're joking! I always thought he was a raving homosexual! Me and my mates, we looked forward to reading his articles in the *Sunday Times* every week.' On came the full theatrical camp. '"Osgood received the ball on the wing, the sweat glistening on his well-formed thigh. He slipped the ball inside to the sturdy Harris who crossed it over to the tall, blonde Burchinall," I mean what are you supposed to think when you read stuff like that but the bloke's a screaming nonce? I used to imagine him sitting up in the press box at Chelsea in a purple turban with long, painted fingernails. "Hello, Office, Glanville here. No, Osgood didn't score today, but he can score with me tonight, whoops!"'

'You've been sussed, you old queen!' I informed Dad that evening.

Tears of mirth streamed down his face; his stomach heaved and he was convulsed, unable to speak for five minutes.

For their first game of the new season United were drawn, conveniently, at Southampton, the nearest First Division football club to Piddlehinton where the family had retired for the summer. Dad, who was reporting the game for the *Sunday Times*, accompanied me on the train journey, turbanless, but with his perennial blue shoulder bag and the obligatory foil-wrapped sandwiches and can of beer. Dorset's narcotic air seemed to have taken the edge off his usual travelling angst, and the journey to Southampton was calm to the point of dullness. It was a rare opportunity to see my team in action. At Oxford I was playing a lot of football, but watching very little. The local side were mired in the quicksand of the League's lower divisions. Only the potential for aggro would spur me aboard the Headington-bound bus, and if Millwall, Portsmouth, or local rivals Swindon were in town, I'd stand alongside their supporters on the away terrace.

As we approached Southampton's ground I spotted Tiger's head. It hadn't occurred to me that I might bump into any of my old sparring partners and I wasn't prepared, but the idea of introducing them to Dad, who'd heard so much about them, appealed. I guessed they weren't *Sunday Times* readers and there'd be little chance they'd know who he was, let alone have fantasised about his press-box attire, so I bounded after them.

'Oy, Tiger!'

He didn't notice me at first and scowled in the general direction of my voice. When he did see me, I wasn't sure if he was going to embrace or thump me, such was the preconditioned aggression of his response to any form of excitement. Dad, who'd caught us up, looked anxious.

'Fuck me! 'Ere, look 'o it ain't!' Tiger grinned. The pleasant feeling of warmth I felt at his acceptance was tinged with guilt at my betrayal of it.

'I'd given ap! I saved all the programmes for yer, 'omes, aways, the lot, didn' I, Coco?'

This touched me almost to tears.

'But I fought you wasn't camin' back, so I sold 'em all last week. 'Ere, you gonna join us then?'

'I'm sitting with me old man.'

Dad nodded and smiled irritably. I knew he was keen to be in the ground.

'That's awright. Good to see yer mate, anyway.'

I shook hands with the rest of the old firm who smiled and asked no questions. The game, a 1–1 draw, was as undramatic as our meeting; nothing impinged on the cosiness of the west country cocoon, and Dad and I returned with time for a game of ping-pong in the beech-shadowed garden before dusk walked off with the last evening light.

* * *

There was no garden to cultivate in our student digs on Cowley Road; not even a window-box, which was probably just as well, since it was hard enough just to keep the house in order. We had a rota for cleaning, cooking and washing-up, not to mention the fact that rent now had to be paid and bills met. Real life had begun. Nothing could stave off the chill wind that twisted up the staircase. Rotten, single-paned sash windows and lethargic storage heaters barely reversed its effects. The fridge was the warmest place in the house. Even in October we'd go to bed fully clothed, in hats and scarves to boot. Tim and I wore football scarves, Ben and Graham college ones, which summed up the house divide. Oxford was a place to which Tim and I were content to be affiliated but unhappy to be seen to belong. Students didn't own college scarves. The college scarves owned the students just as surely as those of Man United and Watford owned me and Tim.

Term began auspiciously with the arrival of Millwall. Tim came along with me, and we watched it go off after the game as the league's most notorious fans took on the locals, though the ritualised confrontation with its stylised swings and kicks was more amusing than alarming. I guessed Tim, who'd found the house and chosen its tenants, had selected me for my laddish credentials.

Communal life at 251A was conducted around the dinner

table, next to the kitchen where most of us were learning to cook for the first time. My brother's gift of *The Multidish Cook-book* turned out to be a poisoned chalice, each of its recipes either lacking a key ingredient or adding a superfluous one. Working in league with it was the 'fast' electric casserole dish, courtesy of Mum, that had barely the capacity to feed two small children. After two hours a plate of cold lamb served with potatoes and severely al-dente leeks would appear. Sometimes this was followed by what became known as 'Mile Island Fool'. I generally forgot to allow the fruit sufficient time to cool before blending in the painstakingly whipped cream, with the result that gooseberry fool turned to gooseberry soup.

I was a lone arts student among scientists and soon discovered they worked much longer hours than I did, returning each evening with open beaks.

'Come on Glanville! We're starving!' was an oft-heard refrain, usually led by Ben's high tenor. Cooking had turned me into the house fool, and I expanded my role with surreal humour and magic routines that always went wrong. But in Ben I found a rival for top billing at the dinner table. He was unhappy with the status his degree course bestowed on him. The less vocational and more abstract your course at Oxford, the greater your kudos. Thick and Chemist went together like horse and carriage. So to boost his credentials Ben specialised in putting down, as vehemently as possible, the thing he was.

'I've just been down The Stoat and Weasel for sixteen pints of Thruxton's Quadruple Metallurgist, spilt most of it, mind, and I've thrown up eight times already, but I can still taste the yeast through the carrots.'

His patter grew and developed, honed with constant repetition. But where Ben's humour was driven, overwhelming its
audience with manic intensity, mine relied on sympathy.

No one in the house had a girlfriend, but we had regular
female company. An old schoolmate of Ben's was going out
with Minty, a student at the Poly, whose friends needed
somewhere to stay in Oxford over the long vacation. Ben
offered them 251A. They continued to come round after
term had begun, and blunted the edge of the all-male
atmosphere.

Minty and her boyfriend turned up one evening when I was
cooking. Walking into the living room, I felt as if I'd been
winded. Araminta. Her name marked her out as a regular in
Jennifer's Diary. She was far too attractive and poised ever
to be interested in someone like me. Her voice was well
modulated but gentle, not what I'd expected. I wondered
whether her reserve stemmed from shyness rather than
arrogance. There was nothing I would have changed about
her. Her green eyes sparkled with fun, and her short blonde
hair added a teasing touch of boyishness to her very feminine
appearance.

While I was confined to the kitchen, captive to the slowest
oven in the world, I heard Ben go into the manic rhythm
of his Metallurgist sketch. Whereas I was overfamiliar with
it, his guests seemed to be hearing it for the first time, and,
much to my irritation, were soon helpless with laughter.
Worse was to follow. *The Multidish Cookbook*'s Pata' all'
angelo with its mouth-watering double cream, grated mature
cheddar, tomatoes and chopped onions all blended with potato

lovingly removed from and restored to its jacket had gone horribly wrong. What had sounded fit for the gods was rendered tasteless by the cookbook's traditional superfluous ingredient, in this case egg white, which managed to neutralise every other flavour. I salted it, peppered it, added knobs of cheese and butter, but it was hopeless.

'God, Glanville!' Ben chuckled, 'we were just about to go out and buy your guests fish and chips. May I introduce them? I think it's some time since you've met.'

Mortified by the impending culinary disaster, my tongue was paralysed.

'Thanks. I'm starving!'

'Yes, Minty. I think we all are!' chuckled Ben. 'Well, now it's here, let's get on with it. He who hesitates is lost.'

'He who has his cakes is lost?' I pretended to mishear. Ben looked at me quizzically.

'Mark, are you sure you're alright?'

I felt betrayed. A silence ensued during which the food was attacked, and for a moment I thought I might get away with it.

'Mark, what exactly have you put in this?' asked Tim.

Even my allies were restless.

'It's potato stuffed with potato!' trumpeted Graham, the little boy bold enough to state that the Emperor really wasn't wearing any clothes.

After dinner Ben held court from beneath his duvet in the vast room he'd won in the ballot. A fan heater blew constantly beneath it, roasting his testicles like chestnuts, as he rattled off yet another version of the Metallurgist sketch, with a new twist to keep his audience's attention. After another jibe at physicists, Graham, who was one, went to bed, but Araminta seemed to have had a wonderful time, despite the potato stuffed with potato. The more of her I took in, the more sensitive and vulnerable she seemed. To kiss her must be like biting through chocolate into cream. But as she was someone else's, I'd have an excuse for not doing anything about her. Coming out of a long relationship, its anxieties, jealousies, expectations and proscriptions, was detoxing. Powerful energies were released that had to be trapped and channelled if they weren't to become destructive. Since breaking up with Chrissie I'd felt no impulse to embark on another one, but my encounter with Minty had quite shaken me.

I hoped that the energy involved in putting on a lunch-time recital might have the effect of sublimating some of my re-emerging hormones, and accordingly asked the Pembroke organ scholar to accompany me. He seemed to have forgotten or at least forgiven my failings as a chorister and agreed to play for me. Pembroke's panelled Oak Room with its magnificent Steinway grand was the perfect concert venue. I chose songs which created an emotional response in me that I hoped to bounce back onto my audience. I began with Stradella's *Pieta Signore,* which, according to tradition, the composer extemporised as he was waylaid by a gang of robbers intent on murdering him.

Have pity, Lord, on my sorrowing.
If my prayer should reach you,
Don't punish me,
Look upon me mercifully,
And don't let me be damned to eternal hellfire.

Such was the beauty of Stradella's song, it's said, the robbers downed weapons and wept. I gave myself over to its emotional truth, heedless of a voice that sometimes failed me at the top. My programme wasn't polished, I missed a few entries, the rubato was indulgent, the tuning sometimes flat, but the audience of Fellows and professors seemed moved, chiefly, I guessed, because my complete lack of interest in anything technical left me unfettered by any consciousness of process that might interfere with my ability to communicate. I sometimes wondered how precarious my position at Oxford might be, in view of my many misdemeanours, some of which the college must have known about (there was no shortage of spies) but from that day onwards I had an important ally – Sir Geoffrey Arthur, the Master of Pembroke, who was passionate about music and singing.

* * *

Back in London for the vacation, Problem found me a job stripping wallpaper with Bindi, an unemployed Indian actress. The original strippers, one of whom I discovered was Edwin, my Geordie friend, had removed most of it, leaving only the difficult pieces where the wall and ceiling joined at the picture-rail. It was nasty, sweaty work, not helped by the despotic nature of our employer, who yelled at us for leaving windows open, and refused to let us take our lunch in the house or receive phone calls.

One morning I heard her instructing her nanny to pack for Dorset.

'Have you got a house in Dorset?'

'Yes. Why do you want to know?' she responded haughtily.

'Because I have too.'

'Oh! Do your family come from there?' she smiled patronisingly.

'No.'

'Did you live there?'

'No.'

'Then why do you have a house there?'

'It's my family's holiday home.'

'Oh!'

She seemed so shocked that her lowly wallpaper stripper might come from a two-home family that Bindi and I worked out a revenge strategy. She would ask me questions about a fictitious house in Tuscany, which I would answer as loudly and fully as possible in our employer's hearing. It didn't take long.

'Did I hear you say you have a house in Tuscany as well?' she asked, peering round a door as another lump of paper tumbled onto my head.

'Yes.'

'Oh! How wonderful! Is it close to the sea?'

'No, but that doesn't matter, 'cos we've got an outdoor swimming pool and a tennis court. It's great!'

'Oh, how super! Where is it exactly?'

'A little village called Romper Coglione, near Arezzo. Do you know it?'

'I'm afraid I don't.'

She wouldn't. I'd chosen the Italian phrase for 'bollock-breaker', the one I felt most readily applied to her.

'And do you find it difficult to look after it?'

'No. We have someone who comes in regularly to keep an eye on things, a Signora Stronzo.'

I felt sure she wouldn't know the Italian for Mrs Shit.

'And do you ever rent it out?'

'Only to relatives and very close friends.'

'Oh, that's a shame. My mother would love to go back there.'

'Is she Italian?'

'Lord, no! British as the flag!'

By the time I left it had become almost embarrassing.

'We must have you back. I'll give you something nicer to do next time. A spot of gardening.'

Bindi received no such offer, but our little fraud had bonded us and I was flattered by her suggestion that she come and see me when term began.

* * *

Back in Oxford, things had changed. The good news was that Minty had split with her boyfriend, the bad that she was now going out with a member of the hated Officer Training Corps. I wasn't surprised. It was common for the posher Oxford Poly students to become involved with the forces boys who generally shared a similar social background. Ben and other predators hovered over the carcass of her dead relationship, confident that this new one wouldn't last either.

Within days I bumped into her cycling down Cowley Road, my tweed coat aflap, trousers tucked inside socks, red and white burnous wrapped round my neck, the whole incongruous outfit framed by a bowler hat, and the monkey boots that had seen service with the Cockney Reds.

'You can't go to a tutorial dressed like that!'

Before I could explain that my sole consideration was to shut out the chill spring air on the two mile trip into college, she preempted me.

'You've got odd socks on.'

'The rest all need darning.'

'I'll do them for you.'

The sun was suddenly shining.

* * *

Bindi arrived as she'd promised. I picked her up at the station and at first barely recognised her, away from the familiar context of work. For a start she was wearing a black dress rather than the red and white striped dungarees I was used to. It was the sort of dress a five year-old might wear to a party, with straps over the shoulders, flouncy at the bottom, and with a yellow teddy bear embroidered on the front. Underneath it she wore white tights and shiny black patent leather shoes with silver buckles. It had a curious, and quite alienating, schoolgirl fantasy effect, and I wondered whether people who saw us might think I was a paedophile.

'Do you like my dress? It makes me look like Alice,' she announced proudly.

I whisked her out of the glare of the platform striplights and into a dark corner of *Maxwell's*. Once our burgers were in front of us I felt more at ease. She warned me that we might get some funny reactions, an Indian girl with a white boy, not just from white racists but Indians.

'Mum's practically cut off by her family because of Dad. He's dead now, but it makes no difference.'

'Were they different castes?'

'No. He was white.'

It wasn't an unfamiliar situation. Dad's mother had referred to my half-Jewish Mum as 'that woman', and made it very clear how unhappy she was about his involvement with her.

'What do you feel you are yourself?'

'Jewish. One hundred per cent.'

I admitted that despite being constantly reminded of my Jewish background throughout childhood and strongly feeling that it defined me, according to orthodox law I wasn't actually Jewish.

'It makes me feel very rootless. What about you?'

'I don't think it matters. I know what I am, I'm both. It just means that everyone can hate me. That's why I wanted to warn you.'

Back at the house I wooed her with two-tone and soul. I heard Graham engaging her in smalltalk as she made her way downstairs to the loo. She reappeared, transformed by a broad smile.

'You're not a football hooligan!'

'Who said I was?'

'Graham. He says you can't decide whether you're an opera singer or a football hooligan and actually you're neither.'

'Thanks pal.'

'Are you?'

I never felt comfortable about seduction, partly because I always expected to be rejected but also because, inexplicably, I felt as if I were committing a crime. I closed my eyes, detaching myself from the arm that was draped round her non-committally, absolving myself of all responsibility for what was about to happen; offering her the opportunity to take the bait but at the same time leaving windows of possibility open if she didn't. Bindi suddenly looked very anxious.

'I'm not very experienced. You'll have to show me what to do.'

I hadn't even really thought about what I was going to do, but now it seemed natural to kiss her so I did, lowering her down onto the floor gently, as if she were an injured bird, taking an eternity over each stage so as not to alarm her. She looked wounded. I was a little unnerved by the parental feelings she excited in me, and my sexual intentions felt wrong. As I undressed her, I felt as if I were preparing a sick patient for bed. I tried to ignore the terrible scarring on the insides of her thighs. We moved onto the bed. Bindi's responses were unspontaneous and mechanical, and when I tried to have intercourse with her, her muscles contracted to form an impenetrable barrier, and her face creased and twisted, but with pain rather than pleasure.

'I'm sorry, Mark. I'm not very good at this.' Her eyes were filled with anxiety. 'Listen, there's something else I should tell you.'

I wondered how many more provisos there were to be.

'I was in a psychiatric home for five years. I used to mutilate myself. Look!'

She showed me her wrists where the skin was knotted from what must have been a ferocious suicide attempt, and the scars on her thighs I'd noticed earlier.

'I did it with a razor blade. They had to graft skin from my buttocks.'

There were scars there too, but they were neater, scored with care.

'You won't want to have anything to do with me now, will you?'

I kissed her, but it felt like a gesture. Inside I felt uncomfortably empty.

'My dungarees, you know I wear them to look like a teddy bear,' she smiled. 'It makes me feel secure. My mother used to say she'd fallen in love with my father because he was a great big teddy bear!'

We spent the night cuddling. Bindi held me more tightly than anyone ever had, as if she wanted to be inside me.

She came to my twenty-first birthday party, which I gave because I felt I had to. Matt turned up halfway through and walked off with most of the booze, just to prove he didn't discriminate. As one large group arrived another would leave with the result that there never seemed to be more than thirty people at any given time, a paltry number for a room as large as Ben's, and since it was his room he could call the shots. He turned off the hi-fi and went to bed not much after midnight, forcing the rest of us to follow suit.

Sexually things hadn't progressed, although Bindi and I went through the motions of lovers. That night, as I lay beside her, she began to jerk and convulse. I called her but she didn't seem conscious, and when I touched her, her body had become completely rigid. Every muscle had contracted and she was starting to spasm. I carefully massaged each part of her and as I did so the muscles relaxed. She hadn't woken. I went to sleep but awoke to find her rigid again and convulsing much more violently than before, as if she were possessed. Now nothing I could do to relax her had any effect. I was in a dilemma. I couldn't possibly leave her like this, but if I called an ambulance I wondered what on earth they'd think to find a girl in my bed in such a state. I also had to consider that by involving them I might be causing her to be reincarcerated in the sort of institution she was so glad to have escaped. But there was no real choice. Our payphone wasn't working, so I was forced to dress and make a call from the box outside the pub opposite. The arrival of ambulance men shocked Bindi into semi-consciousness, and she began to cry, which at least showed that she was registering the situation. They told me she'd been in a catatonic trance and that if there were no significant improvement within an hour they'd be forced to take her in.

'How could you do this? You know my history!' she sobbed, still not in control of her body. 'Get my address book. It's in my coat. Look under "M" and you'll see the name of my psychiatrist, Margaret.'

It was late morning but inside the house nothing was moving. The debris of empty wine bottles, crisps and half-eaten sandwiches added to my desolation. A queue had formed outside the call-box and an animated girl was gabbling away interminably. As I waited a middle-aged woman crossed the road, stood outside the pub and produced a large, white handkerchief that she held at each corner and began bowing up and down, all the while intoning 'The Grand Master will get ye!' a mantra she punctuated with banshee-like shrieks.

I called Margaret's number and a soft, lentil-bake voice answered. I told her I was a friend of Bindi's and that I thought she'd had some sort of breakdown.

'Oh, shit! Tell me. What did she have to eat last night?'

'I think it was a hamburger.'

'Hamburger. Okay, and did Bindi have a bun with the burger?'

'I think so.'

'Chips?'

'Yeah.'

'Side salad.'

'Can't remember.'

It was like ordering a takeaway.

'To drink?'

'Coke, I think.'

'Right . . .'

I was distracted. The handkerchief lady had returned, this time carrying an empty bottle which she hurled through the pub window with a crash and an exultant cry. I was forced to ask Margaret to repeat herself.

'Right. What I was saying is that in the case of someone like Bindi it's almost certainly the bun.'

'The bun?'

'Right. The wheat segments in the bun that she had with the burger. It can tip the balance.'

Now I knew. I looked up and down uninspiring Cowley Road, searching for a piece of ballast to anchor me in a world spinning out of control.

Back in the house, *On My Radio* was playing loudly. Graham emerged from his bedroom and looked confused.

'I was just coming to tell you to shut the fuck up, but you're here.'

I had to tell someone about my terrible night.

'Hang on, now let me get this straight. While I've been asleep there's been a naked girl upstairs in a catatonic trance, ambulance men, and a mad woman across the road attacking an Irish pub with a bottle. Could have done with a bit more of that at the party!'

He poked me in the chest.

I opened the door to my bedroom, with some trepidation, to find a fully dressed Bindi sifting through my record collection. She gave me a big smile. She seemed to have made an astonishingly swift recovery, and I began to wonder whether Margaret's diagnosis hadn't been right. We spent the rest of the day listening to music, in particular a frenetic punk version of *You're Ready Now* by a Manchester group called Slaughter and the Dogs. By evening I felt it was safe to leave her for a couple of hours while I went for a much needed drink with Tim.

We returned to find the house in darkness and a very worried Graham.

'Thanks for that.'

'For what?'

'For leaving me on me own in the house with her. She's just played that Slaughter and the Dogs record seventeen and a half consecutive times.'

He showed me a piece of paper scored with as many lines.

'And a half?'

'Half way through the eighteenth time, yeeeep! Then I hear her coming down the stairs. I was trembling in me room! She could've had a knife.'

Bindi stayed the night, but when I woke she'd gone, without leaving a trace. Later in the day she phoned from a hotel in Oxford, wouldn't say which, and told me she was fine. I never saw her or heard from her again. She'd met me too young: I was still too much in need of parenting myself to cope with those needs in others.

* * *

Another who'd faded from the scene recently was Matt, along with the Table Six Crew. They'd been forced to give in to the demands of Finals and thoughts of a world beyond Oxford. Fruit and game machines were still emptied regularly, but the lads were going through a Robin Hood phase. Matt was raising money for an Oxford University Athletics Club tour by selling badges at thirty pence a time, while Harry was flogging copies of *Cherwell*, where he was features editor, for twenty pence a throw. No one bothered that the substantial income each obtained from selling these items bore no relation to the quantities sold.

The clans were to gather for the last time on the day of Matt's Finals celebrations. These festivities, which had been banned by Oxford City council the previous year, arguably constituted the single greatest affront to the town. Drunken students would spend a week firing champagne corks at cars and buses travelling up and down the busy High Street, and rampage round its vicinity. This year the ban had been lifted, and the united firms of Pembroke, Worcester and New College assembled to greet Matt, each carrying a bottle of brown ale supplied by Harry the Scouser, a suitably proletarian alternative to the champagne whose spray clouded the air and rained down on us as the hero emerged. Glancing behind, Harry identified the source as a bunch of Monday Clubbers, ultra-right-wing Tories we considered mortal enemies. Matt, puffing on a fag, shook up a bottle of the brown, walked up to the principal celebrant, and unleashed its sweet, sticky liquid into his ruddy-cheeked complexion. Going even ruddier in his anger, the hapless Tory began shaking his bottle of Moet, accidentally catching Matt on the side of the face with it as he did so. Matt grabbed him by his lapels, hauled him off the ground and round the corner from the Examination Schools into Merton Street. Then, without giving him a chance to remonstrate, Matt head-butted his open, unsuspecting face. I heard a loud crack. Blood gushed out of his nose and all over his shirt as he stood there in total bewilderment, a red rivulet working its way down his chin, repeating 'Who are you? Who the hell are you?' as we disappeared up Merton Street. It was the most gratuitous piece of violence I'd witnessed at Oxford, cruelly certain to cause maximum damage and the fitting conclusion to an Oxford career that had been stained throughout by crime and bloodshed; yet I couldn't help but empathise with Matt, even though the little he betrayed of himself meant that I never understood him, and when I looked at him it was a distorted reflection of myself that stared back.

* * *

Towards the end of term Moira, a friend of Minty's, decided that I would be the perfect chaperone to escort herself, Jackie, and, I could scarcely believe it, Minty herself, to the south of Spain. Minty was currently on her second officer, but here was the best possible opportunity. Not that I would have readily turned down any trip to Spain, least of all in the company of three attractive girls.

Mijas is a small Moorish town on the western Costa del Sol. From a distance it looks like a cluster of cardboard

boxes painted white. Our apartment belonged to Moira's
aunt. Situated half way down a set of narrow stone steps,
it comprised a small room, a large room and a bathroom.
Inside it was dark and sparsely furnished but the window in
the main room opened onto a panorama of parched, barren
country stretching to the horizon.

There was a beach, but it was more accessible by car than
foot. Fine, hot sand extended thirty yards from the sea to
the road, and continued as far as the eye could see. I
was embarrassed about revealing my pasty white body in
the midst of so many bronzed ones but I wasn't alone.
Although Minty seemed to have a naturally deeper colour
than the rest of us, Jackie and Moira were as white as a
fish's underbelly. Out came the high-factor sun-creams and
the towels. Moira produced an enormous white, floppy canvas
hat and procured herself a deck chair where she sat and read
a Harold Robbins novel.

'Fancy a swim, anyone?' Minty called.

Turning round, I saw she'd stripped down to a sapphire-
blue bikini. I watched her skipping over the sand, Jackie
following close behind her.

'I'm afraid it's a bit hot for me,' Moira said from underneath
her hat. She was still in her blouse and cotton trousers. 'It's
not really my cup of tea this climate.'

'I don't think it's going to get much cooler.'

'Oh dear! Do you think so?' she laughed good-naturedly.
'Well, Minty and Jackie seem to be enjoying it.'

'Jackie's a nice girl.'

'Hmm.'

'Not so keen?'

'I don't trust her. You know she really pushed Araminta

to let her come on this holiday. I mean, we don't really know her, and Araminta's so good-natured, she can't say no.'

'Well, I'm just glad you asked me.'

'Oh, you're alright. Minty really likes you.'

The sun on my back felt cold in comparison with the tingling glow inside me. I let the sound of the sea lull me into a semi-slumber that was interrupted by the vibration of pounding feet coming back up the beach. Cool droplets of water fell onto my back. Minty was shaking her hair. Jackie lifted her towel to flick off the sand which caught in the wind and blew back, annoyingly, onto me.

The following day, left alone with Minty for the first time, I asked her about her split with Chris, and the two OTC boyfriends she'd had since. She went into fairly graphic detail.

'Hamish was strange. He never wanted to make love. I started to think there was something wrong with me . . .'

'Hardly!' I interrupted, speedily regretting it.

'No, I could make him come, but he wouldn't fuck me.'

The thought of Minty making someone come, and how she'd achieved it. My mind was invaded by a multitude of lurid images. I tried desperately to keep my face blank.

'And what about Ben?' I asked.

'Oh, he's so sweet, don't you think?'

'He is with you.'

'Mmm, he is rather keen,' she giggled. 'Poor Ben,' and then she was convulsed with sudden laughter.

'One day I came round to your house . . .'

'Yes.'

'Well, actually, I'd come to see Tim. We were going to play tennis . . .'

'And?'

'And Ben answered the door, completely starkers, except for an exercise book over his genitals!'

'You're joking!'

'He was!'

'How peculiar!'

'I know. It gets worse!' she laughed again. 'He asked me upstairs for a cup of tea. I couldn't refuse, could I?'

'Of course not.'

'Well, he led the way up the stairs and . . .' Minty laughed again, '. . . his buttocks were completely exposed!'

'I see. So the exercise book wasn't large enough to cover his arse.'

'I don't know. He didn't try.'

'Sweet of him.'

'Yes, wasn't it! But worst of all, he had an enormous birthmark on his right buttock. It was horrible,' and she went off into convulsions again. 'I've had nightmares since, about Ben trying to seduce me with a great hairy posterior . . .'

'His own, I hope! Does he have a hairy rump?'

'Oh no! Only in the dream.'

'Hiyah!' Jackie was back. 'You two seem to be having a good time. Want to share the joke?'

'Oh no, it's nothing. Just something to do with Ben.'

* * *

That night I pondered my next move. If I were to succeed with Minty, one thing was clear: all buttock hair had to be removed. So the next time I had a shower I shaved my backside. The following morning, horror of horrors, it was covered in a rash of unsightly red pimples, alongside which Ben's birthmarked bum would look like a Botticelli masterpiece. It would set me back a while.

*   *   *

Mijas's charms soon wore off. Its beach, bar, bed routine quickly became monotonous. I longed to escape it and visit other places with more history, architecture and, quite frankly, romance. Neither Moira nor Jackie seemed particularly taken with the prospect of a trip to Granada but Minty was.

Mijas's geographical isolation and almost non-existent public transport meant we'd have to hitch there. By the time we arrived it was dusk. We made inquiries at a couple of pensions but they were either full or too expensive, and we ended up sleeping beneath the walls of the Alhambra, on a small patch of hard, dark soil where the ants didn't seem too numerous and lizards darted to and fro. It was dusk and a dusty, lemony smell hung in the air. I lay down on the bare earth with a rucksack beneath my head and, to my delight, Minty lay down beside me and placed her head on my chest. A warm feeling flowed through my stomach, exacerbated by a spontaneous surge in the groin that I hoped she hadn't noticed. I kissed her hair and smelt her essence for the first time. She didn't respond but left her head where it was. I didn't want to spoil the day by being rebuffed, so I tried to sleep, concentrating on the sound of running water, as total darkness submerged us.

I couldn't sleep. I was in torment. Here we were in a setting of high romance, yet I felt the barriers were still raised. For now the best option seemed to let things be and hope that the castle's charms might aid me. The next morning nothing was said about the previous night.

Returning, it became increasingly clear that all was far from won. I cared so much for her that I found the courage to be more direct than I'd ever been before as our train chugged through the barren lowlands beneath the Sierra Nevada.

'Do you think we could have a relationship?'

'Well I like you a lot.'

'But?'

'I think you're hard.'

Had she heard about my days with the Cockney Reds, or my misdemeanours with Matt and the Table Six Crew? I asked her what she meant.

'That poor Indian girl. You just dumped her.'

'That's the last thing I did.'

I tried to explain what had happened, but as I did so, I began to question my behaviour, and the fact that I hadn't tried to contact Bindi since that terrible weekend. Minty seemed to have been given a version which placed me in the worst possible light. Someone had attempted to ensure that she and I would never get together. The more I tried to justify myself, the more I found myself engaged in a slanging match. Strangely, it felt as if we were two lovers rowing, so there was an undoubted intimacy between us, which in itself was encouraging. Certain obstacles must have fallen without my even being aware of it.

Back in Mijas Moira had become redder, Jackie browner, and the atmosphere in our small apartment darker and more claustrophobic. The time the girls had been left on their own together had focused their differences. Moira, in particular, seemed furious at having been abandoned, even though neither she nor Jackie had shown the least interest in joining our expedition. The divide had the effect of drawing me and Minty closer together, and the bonds of suspicion that held Minty from me began to loosen. She finally allowed me to kiss her. I felt what it meant to Minty as her lips finally parted, but I didn't want to take things too far. I feared losing the advantage I'd gained, not to mention that at any moment we might be caught *in flagrante* by one of the girls. Moira and Jackie's assumptions about our relationship probably didn't match the reality, but it meant they left us a certain amount of time and space. Like guilty teenagers we'd snatch embraces wherever these moments occurred, whether on the carousel, or out in the still warm sea. When the sun set at eight, the moon brushed a silver channel across the dark water, out of whose reach it was easy to hide while Moira and Jackie walked along the shore, calling to us like worried parents.

I'd tried and failed to book flights for Malaga, so we all ended up returning via Madrid. It meant spending a night in an hotel. Unprompted, Minty booked us into a double room, so at last we had privacy, but still the course did not run smooth.

'You *are* callous.'

'What have I done?'

'You were going to fuck me.'

It was only the second time I'd heard her use the word. Pronounced so gently, so aristocratically, it tasted as it never had, acrid-sweet like the scent beneath the walls of the Alhambra. All my sensations and experiences were heightened and sharpened in her presence, and I felt despair that she still wasn't mine, that at a moment such as this I might lose her.

'I'm not on the pill and you're not protected, but you don't care.'

I couldn't explain the overwhelming urge to have sex with her, that overrode my every consideration and brooked no opposition, and just lay beside her silently worrying. It was the start of our non-communication.

* * *

The start of the new university year found Minty on the dole in London, exiled from Oxford, but with the excuse of a new relationship to make her a frequent returnee. One morning, as we lay in bed, I traced my finger down her back, from the base of her neck where her soft hair fell, down to the crevice between her buttocks, white against the fading summer tan, little by little applying more pressure, each time taking the finger slightly lower, until it was brushing down between her legs, urging her to turn round, grab me, fuck me, but her spine remained rigid, her buttocks clamped shut, her thighs tautened.

'Minty!'

She didn't answer.

'Minty, what is it?'

I ran through the events of the past twenty-four hours in my mind. Everything seemed to be in place. I couldn't imagine why she should be annoyed or upset.

'Minty, what's wrong?'

'You know perfectly well.'

'But what?'

'You're so fucking selfish.'

'In what way?'

'You know.'

'I don't.'

'Of course, you do. You make me sick!'

'Please tell me what it is.'

'You know full well.'

'I don't, or I wouldn't be asking you. Please tell me what I've done.'

'I can't.'

'What do you mean.'

'Well, if you don't think there's anything wrong then there's no point discussing it.'

I wracked my brain to try to work out what on earth was wrong.

'Minty, please tell me,' I hoped she'd hear the smile in my voice since she had her back to me. 'Minty, please!'

'What's the point talking about it?'

'Talking about what?'

'Minty, I love you.'

'You can't do.'

'I do do.'

'Then why don't you make love to me properly.'

'What do you mean *properly*?'

'Well, you know.' She placed my hand on the spot I vainly imagined I'd been visiting regularly for the last three months. 'What? Do you mean you had no idea?'

'Have I ever actually?'

'Not that I remember.'

This was extraordinary. Bindi's frigidity had so damaged my sexual confidence that I was grateful simply to have found an accepting entrance. It hadn't occurred to me that it might have been the wrong one.

The utter absurdity of it all suddenly hit me, and I was convulsed with laughter.

'You really didn't know?'

'No.'

The tears were streaming down my face, and now Minty was laughing too.

'Did you ever come?'

'Sometimes.'

'Oh, Minty!'

We burst out laughing again.

'Let's do it properly. If you'd told me . . .'

She took me in her sensual hands and steered me between her legs, homewards, and into the goal I thought I'd reached three months before. How different it felt now, embracing me completely, willing me towards the orgasm I had so rarely attained, until we were both lost in this timeless, fantastic fuck.

* * *

'Mark, have you met Geoffrey Sweet, our new Junior Dean yet?' asked Godfrey, the newly elected senior Dean. 'Awfully nice chap and a first-rate pianist, I hear. I think he's quite keen to meet you.'

Geoffrey Sweet was currently Public Enemy Number One in Pembroke thanks to his habit of attending JCR meetings uninvited; relations with him might well be construed as betrayal. I suspected myself that the college had brought him in as a hatchet man, expected to make full use of the powers his title bestowed, hence his presence at the meetings. The

Table Six Crew, myself included, who'd always been at the centre of unrest, must surely be a prime target. But if this was the case, they'd mistimed it. Only Andy and myself were left. With the departure of Harry the Scouser and his Worcester accomplice, the reign of terror had come to an end.

He had a suite in the MacMillan building, no doubt to keep him in touch with the students he was meant to be supervising. Like all rooms there, it was functional and warm, sufficient to his needs. His appearance made it very hard to perceive him as a threat, but I wondered whether that mightn't have made him more of one. A tiny, fair-haired cherub with ruddy cheeks and perfect features, he would not have looked out of place on the ceiling of a Florentine church, except, if you looked closely, you might detect the etchings of life on his forehead and around his eyes. He ushered me to a chair and filled a couple of tumblers with Pembroke's finest. I was fascinated to see miniatures of Marx and Lenin keeping watch over a selection of their works. My mind filled with possibilities of double and treble espionage (the Master of the College — and his ultimate boss — was suspected of being a recruiter for MI6), but, if that were so, surely he wouldn't be so indiscreet as to advertise the fact.

'Oh! Do you like them? I got them in Leipzig.'

'Leipzig?'

'That's where I spent my year out.'

'Wasn't that a strange choice? Wouldn't it have been more fun to go to Berlin or, I don't know, Munich?'

'Why? Everyone goes there. I wanted to do something different. Besides, have you any idea how cheap music is in East Germany? More sherry?'

I'd finished the first tumbler without even realising it. Was I being softened for some horrible sting? At any moment cupboards might fly open, and out would spring proctors and dons with warrant sheets.

'Was it?'

'Oh, you wouldn't believe it, Mark! I bought the entire keyboard output of Bach, Beethoven, Liszt, Chopin and Schubert for under twenty pounds.'

I then discovered he was a concert pianist who'd turned down a music college scholarship to study French and German at New College, a footballer who had been on Glasgow Rangers' books as a junior, and a junior Fellow at his old college who'd just been appointed Junior Dean of mine.

'I'm beginning to regret it, Mark. You were there for that JCR meeting.' He'd noticed me. 'I mean, did you see the way they were? So disrespectful. I mean, I think I've got every right to attend those meetings, don't you?'

He spoke with the petulance of an affronted child. It suited his appearance and made him much easier to deal with. He seemed as much of a double-agent as I was a hardcore football hooligan, but I still had to be diplomatic. I told him that technically JCR meetings were for undergraduates, and that there was nothing they liked better than to blinkeredly follow their own rules, omitting to add that they'd created this one just to exclude him from the meetings.

'Listen, I've heard great reports about you from Godfrey. He thinks very highly of your singing.' He was aping the clipped, considered speech of the old school don. 'We really ought to do something together.'

So we did. I'd already given a couple of smaller scale concerts in the college, but now I was working alongside someone with University-wide ambitions. For our venue we chose the Holywell Room, the oldest assembly hall in the country, at the heart of the University. Sadly Mark Raphael, the inspiration for our programme and whose own songs I had included, would not be there to hear or prepare me for the recital. He had been cruelly struck by cancer of the throat, which afflicted him in the place his life had centred, the instrument of his expression. It hurt to witness Rayful Mark cut down. I knew I'd never find another like him, but as we rehearsed it became glaringly apparent that there was still a lot of work to do on my voice. Marjorie, my *schutzengel*, suggested a new and very different maestro who came in the shape of John Dalby, a tall, well-built man with a shock of blondish hair and a dazzling grin. We met at the Wigmore Hall studios where he had a room next to Kiri te Kanawa's teacher, Vera Rosza. Mark hadn't interfered with my natural sound, so although the basic quality was fine, it was still immature, a matter John felt had to be rectified.

'Look at that tongue!' he commanded in a camp, high-pitched voice of the school of Kenneth Williams. 'Look at it! Go on, look at it! Sing "Ah." It's like a great fat slug in there. Now point it, point it, that's right, right between those labia. Whooh!'

It seemed to me that as my tongue became flatter the sound grew harsher and when he had me reaching for the top 'A' in *Ich Grolle Nicht*, emitting a cry like a woman in the last throes of labour, I wondered what on earth Vera Rosza must be thinking. My impertinent tongue wasn't the only problem.

'I'll have you knocking that grand piano across the room with your diaphragm by the time I've finished with you!' Before I could react, I was bent over it, John behind me, hand tightly clasping my idle stomach in what I imagined must have looked like a classic position for sodomy to anyone walking in. As I left, a group of young women trooped in and assembled in a line. After introducing us with impeccable etiquette he informed them, 'Mark's just had his first lesson, so he's only just finding out what it means to study with such a wicked taskmaster! Right girls. How are those tits today? Ooh! They're almost as undisciplined as your tongue,' he grinned at me. 'Now come on . . . that's better . . . ,' and he walked down the line, arranging and lifting them while they laughed and smiled. The contrast with Mark Raphael could not have been greater, but as the day of the concert drew nearer, I felt my voice had improved significantly.

It was an amateur programme; too long and demanding, but I'd selected songs and arias that moved me or meant something to me, so I was able to sustain the programme with emotional intention and commitment. It helped that I was playing to a home audience – Mum and Dad were there, my tutor Godfrey Bond, Minty, the Cowley Road gang. Even the Table Six Crew were well represented, something which became apparent at the end as I came out for my encore and was met by a sound like the one that greets United walking out at Old Trafford. Even Matt, still hanging around Oxford, had turned up.

We had a little party back at Cowley Road, attended, somewhat to my concern, by Godfrey, my tutor and Dean.

I feared he might notice various items that had been removed from different outposts of Pembroke, but he simply raised his glass to a plaque marking the erection of the sports pavilion: 'Nice to see you have a small part of Pembroke here!'

One upshot of the concert was an invitation from the Dean of New College to have dinner with himself and his star pupil Geoffrey Sweet. It was my first experience of High Table. I felt like a traitor at New College, where I knew so many people. By the time the undergraduates had finished their meal we were only moving towards the end of our hors d'oeuvre. I was glad when the students had gone, as the elevated status of High Table, both morally and physically, made eating a performance. Within half an hour of retiring to the Senior Common Room, most of the Fellows, for whom this was only routine, made an exit, leaving the Dean and his two guests to explore the vaults of the New College wine cellar I knew so well. I began to notice that each time the Dean or Junior Dean rose to refill a glass, which was often, they seemed less certain on their feet. In the end they were staggering.

'Another bottle, John?'

'Oh, s-splendid!'

Geoff freed himself from the deep armchair, by now more of a hindrance than a support. He missed his first step and fell halfway to the ground before rescuing himself on a Louis Quinze sidetable and propelling himself into the dangerous, no-bottle land in the centre of the room where there was no support or prop. A terrific explosion outside sent him tumbling to the floor. It was followed by trilling undergraduate laughter.

'John, really this is intolerable. You're the Dean of this college. You ought to do something about it!'

The Dean's relaxed torso stiffened decanally. His brow furrowed. Geoff staggered towards him and the two of them swayed towards the door, supporting each other as best they could. Whilst they were leaving, the banging and shouting increased. I estimated it would take them a good five minutes at the rate they were travelling to reach the errant students. Fifteen minutes later there was alcohol-infused bumbling below. Five minutes later, the door to the Senior Common Room swung open, and in lurched the dynamic duo, still propping each other up.

'I thought you dealt with it admirably, John. *Ad*mirably!' squeaked Geoff, his voice rising ever higher as he spoke.

'Oh, do you think so?'

'Mark, you should have seen him. There were ff-five undergraduates . . . drunk . . . probably . . . letting off bangers. "Did you *know* it's an offence to let off fireworks in the grounds of New College? You must all come to my rooms . . . tomorrow . . . at twelve. I'm going to fine you twenty . . . thousand . . . pounds . . . *each*!"'

* * *

Another invitation resulted from my concert. It came from the thirty-five-year-old divorced cousin of a friend. She wrote me a letter, saying how much she'd enjoyed my singing, and suggested we have lunch when I was next in London. Even if she hadn't been attractive, her mid-thirties, divorcee credentials were mouth-watering, something that had not gone unnoticed by an increasingly jealous Minty. She began walking out on me at parties if she felt I'd spent too long talking to a girl I'd met there. On several occasions I cycled the streets of Oxford looking for her, once even enlisting the help of Tim and his car. At first her jealousy convinced me of how much she had grown to love me and helped to allay my own insecurities, but as time went on her incessant accusations began to tear at the very fabric of our relationship.

Minty's milieu could not have been more alien to the one I'd frequented for the last two years. Through her I met the individuals I'd discarded en masse as my anti-Semitic, right-wing enemy. Her flatmate Melissa had been a member of the Oxford University Rifle Club, as had Melissa's boyfriend, Nick. We'd met on occasion at breakfast in London and talked about football and women. I was flattered by how friendly and welcoming he was but wondered if that wasn't because I was enticed by the attractions of acceptance into yet another club that wouldn't have me as a member.

Invitations followed to Rifle Club dinners, hunt balls, public school reunions, and Sloaney parties in the west country with lots of girls called Pippa, one of whom gave a barn dance in Somerset to celebrate her twenty-first. Ceilidhs and square-dances with their set routines and group involvement to the accompaniment of bland English folk music had never appealed to me. Motown always won over Hoedown. It looked so fearsomely complicated. Everyone else seemed either acquainted with the moves or gifted with choreographic genes I lacked. I found myself dancing in a circle between two men, one of whom was Nick.

'Good Lord, Mark! What are you doing here? You'll give people the wrong idea!'

I grinned sheepishly and threw myself into the error. Whoever I didn't fool, I did fool Minty.

'You're such a bastard!'

'What now?'

'Going off and leaving me like that.'

I failed to convince her it was ineptitude, not annoyance at being dragged to yet another barn dance, that had propelled me in the opposite direction.

Minty was avenged on a traditional skittle alley in the local pub, where many of the guests from the previous night had congregated. We were arranged into two teams. Each time it came to my turn, the ball would slip into a rut and miss the target completely. No one else seemed to be having this problem, just as they'd had no difficulty copying the caller's moves at the dance. At first my side were furious at being landed with the dunce. Eventually, as my turn came round and I emerged from the crowd to miscue for the umpteenth time, my appearance was greeted by cheers and applause, which I returned with bows and salutes. In the end I felt it would have been churlish to ruin everyone's fun by actually hitting the target. On the one occasion I did, my success was greeted by a roar worthy of Old Trafford.

Back in Oxford, I felt like Oscar Wilde's dwarf at the birthday of the Infanta, when he realised that they were laughing at him because he was ugly and not because they loved him. Except I had Minty.

'People treat you as their laughter-goat. I don't think it's fair. I got a real twang.'

'A twang?'

'You know. A twang in the clitoris. It's when I get really angry. Twang! Right there!'

'What do you mean "you know"? How's anyone supposed to guess your strange, Mintyish definition?'

'Well,' she grinned, 'now you know.'

'They're such goys!'

'Careful. I'm a goy too. I'm a shiksa, aren't I?'

'Yes, but as Lenny Bruce said, "there are Jews who are goys and goys who are Jews." You can be Jewish in your outlook.'

'Am I?'

She wasn't, but it didn't matter. I kissed her cheek.

'Do you want to be?'

'I don't know. It would be quite fun, I suppose. Do you want me to be?'

'I just want you to be you.'

'I'm not sure you do.'

'Of course I do. I love you.'

'Then why do you go dancing off in that cavalier manner to the other end of the room?'

'Because I'm not a goy.'

'Because you're a hopeless dancer!'

'Huh! You should see me on the disco floor!'

'I have. It's quite comical!'

She began to laugh uncontrollably.

* * *

My final weeks in Oxford shadowed the run-up to the wedding of Prince Charles and Diana. News of it filled papers and conversations alike, and every self-respecting Socialist had to make a suitable anti-establishment gesture. Mine came in the form of a large purple badge inscribed 'Stuff the Wedding' in almost illegible Gothic letters. As I was about to enter Broadgates Hall for my end-of-year summing up, Godfrey appeared. Without warning, he homed in on my badge, practically wrenching it off my gown in an effort to make out its inscription.

'Oh!' he exclaimed with a mixture of anger and disgust, before storming off into the hall.

At the head of a long table framed by sombre-looking fellows in heavy black gowns sat the Master. His large-framed spectacles dangled from a chain round his neck. Most of my tutors were not based in Pembroke, so suitable surrogates read out their reports. Each one seemed more glowing than the last; Godfrey's generously topping the bill. The Master sat back and smiled.

'Well, Mr Glanville, I'm pleased to see you've found the time to keep up all your academic work when I know you've been so busy with your singing and football. Well done.'

I thanked him and was turning to leave when the voice of Godfrey thundered out.

'Before Mr Glanville goes, a word of caution. In the course of the long vacation he must make it his duty to read the texts, and . . .' he faltered, 'it is my belief that he should take the time to . . . read the texts, and . . . he must read the texts, . . . and thoroughly! And it is my belief that over the next few weeks he should . . . read the texts, and . . . make sure he uses the time to . . . read the texts! He could well come down in Finals! *He's overconfident!*' he crescendoed in an outburst of trembling anger that astonished everyone present. At first I attributed the extraordinary coda to the Paisleyite fury of an Ulsterman at my provocative badge, but the tone of his utterance, and the manner of its delivery had a prophetic conviction. I only partially heeded his advice. After Oxford all I wanted was to win a place on a Vocal Studies course somewhere, and that was where I directed my energies.

* * *

Back home in London one afternoon, trying to juggle with the excess of time I had at my disposal after Oxford's usual intense freneticism, I stood in the drawing room, plucking volumes from the shelves of my parents' over-familiar collection. It was a well-excavated archaeological site where I still hoped to turn up an Aztec brooch. New boys were easily spotted. Their shiny dust-jackets contrasted garishly with the faded cloth of Gerald Kersh and C P Snow. *An English Parnassus*; now this was one I hadn't investigated for a while, unremarkable and chunky, the vermilion of its youth faded to an elderly pink rinse. I opened it; instead of the runic flourish indicating it was yet another of Dad's books, here was one inscribed in Mum's curling feminine letters, Pamela de Boer, her name from her previous marriage. I looked closely at the signature, to see if I could discover anything as to how Mum had been at that time. It was dated 1943, perhaps the year of Diana's birth, the product of Mum's liaison with an American army officer, conceived, delivered and concealed from Oliver, her husband, while he was away fighting. She'd never talked much about her other life, or this half sister.

When the door suddenly opened and Mum appeared, I felt as if I'd been discovered rifling through her private possessions, but she seemed more startled than me.

'You gave me quite a shock! What are you reading? Oh, that old thing! That was mine.'

'Mum, did Oliver ever know about your baby?'

'What on earth makes you ask that now?'

'This.'

I pointed to her signature in the book.

'Pamela de Boer.' She pronounced the name as if it didn't belong to her. 'My God, it's rather ancient, isn't it?' She paused. 'I think of her all the time.'

All the time. Diana wasn't part of another life, but the one Mum was living now, and I had known nothing of it.

'I'd love to know what happened to her, where she's living, whether she's married or happy.'

'I thought you knew.'

'A medium told me she was living in Canada . . .'

She'd breastfed her, bonded with her, then, after heavy pressure from her father, the baby had been taken away for adoption when she was three months old. Mum sobbed deeply and I hugged her, feeling the softness of her cardigan on my face.

'I'm hopeless, aren't I?'

'You're a human being.'

'You're strong, Mark. You have real inner strength.'

'I wish I did.'

'That's your problem. You have no self-belief.'

'I'm fine.'

'You're not. None of us are. We delude ourselves, but we're all neurotic up to here.'

She placed a hand between her head and my chin.

'I'm pretty happy.'

'What's happiness? I'm sixty, and I can count the times I've been happy on the fingers of one hand.'

'Because you don't know what happiness is.'
'Damn right! Do you?'

* * *

Something I always looked forward to in the summer was
my trips with Dad to see Shakespeare in Regent's Park. This
year we exchanged the verdant splendour of NW1 for the
Victorian charms of the Aldwych and the RSC's production
of *The Merchant of Venice*.

'Let's have a drink!'
    'How about that pub?'
    'Somewhere a little further from the theatre.'
    I always forgot the stresses attendant on going anywhere
with Dad. Off we traipsed.
    'There must be a fucking pub . . . must be a fucking
pub . . . must be a fucking pub . . .'
    Walking turned to a trot, then a canter as alcohol-free
premises hurtled by. In the end we'd gone full circle.
    'Ah good! There's a pub!'
    The one he hadn't wanted to go into originally.

Spurning the main entrance as if it were too vulgar, he
headed for a door that looked firmly closed, choosing
a route which took him behind the pavement drinkers
sitting naively at their tables. Smish! Kish! Boing! Tonics
and lagers went flying. They looked on in anger and
astonishment. He hadn't noticed. The next obstacle to
confront him was the sealed door whose handle he shook
and rattled.
    'Fuck!'

He retraced his steps behind the tables, destroying all in his wake that had survived the last offensive, whatever had been foolishly left or replaced by carousers brought up on the adage that lightning doesn't strike twice.

Once inside the pub I headed for the fruit machine, keen to put as much distance as possible between us. Hardly had my first ten pence dropped when I heard my name called across the crowded pub with more volume than a parade ground sergeant could normally muster. If I ignored it, I'd be the only one in the pub who did.

'What would you like to drink?'

'Beer!'

'What?'

'Beer!'

'Beer!'

I returned to the fruit machine, my oasis.

'MAA-AARK! What are you going to drink?'

'Beer! I TOLD YOU!'

'There's three different types!'

The Fates weren't conspiring in my favour; I made my way through the deafened punters to the bar.

'If you hadn't gone off playing that fucking machine; you could have told me straightaway!'

In sooth, I know not why I am so sad;
It wearies me, you say it wearies you

Antonio's opening words should have heralded a few hours of peace. Someone started coughing behind us. Dad whirled round in his seat and glared, one head facing away from the stage amongst hundreds. The entire first half was punctuated by this cough and the accompanying swivel of Dad's angry head.

O! Ten times faster Venus' pigeons fly
To seal love's bonds new-made than they are wont
To keep obliged faith unforfeited

Had he registered this amidst the coughing and twisting?

Before the curtain hit the stage to signal the interval, Dad was out of his seat, faster than a cartoon animal. He reappeared minutes later with a couple of tubs.

'I did it!' he beamed. 'First to the ice creams!'

The smile turned to a grimace as a young tourist sauntered past.

'That's her! That's the one! She ought to be in a fucking hospital, not a theatre!' His voice ascended in anger and volume to assail the ears of someone who, by her lack of reaction, apparently understood neither a word of his nor of Shakespeare's.

Ice creams over and ready for part two, a distinguished elderly couple, smiling and smartly dressed, made their way in gingerly fashion back to their seats, which, to their misfortune, happened to be beyond ours.

'Come along, biddies, come along, biddies, come along, biddies,' muttered Dad, heeling his satchel under his seat.

As we headed for Antonio's redemption, the verse seemed to grow in lyricism and beauty, perhaps because I was at last able to concentrate now the twin distractions of cough and head twist were removed.

The man who hath not music in him
Nor moved is by concord of sweet sound
Is fit for treasons, stratagems and spoils.
The motions of his spirit are dull as night
And his affections dark as Erebus:
Let no such man be trusted

My credo. I looked at Dad, so Jewish sitting there, a prototype Shylock but handsome and, beneath the rage, so sensitive.

Our journey home was less fraught. The play had caused him to reflect.

'The first time I saw it was in 1947. I was still at Charterhouse. I'm afraid I found a lot of similarity between that school and sixteenth-century Venice. Freddie never got over it. Did I tell you about his letter? He'd been to see Paul playing for Bedales against Charterhouse, said he was watching from the ghetto end. Newlands was much worse. I was the only Jew in the school, and God did they let me know it. My poor sister had some special dispensation to study there. They bullied her mercilessly. Imagine it. A little girl. What harm could she do anyone?' He lowered his head and shook it sadly.

A couple of days later I was walking to Holland Park station when I caught sight of Dad with his perennial blue satchel over his shoulder. He'd concealed himself behind a phone box, and was peering round it at an old black tramp sitting on a bench in a filthy duffle coat. The tramp one of several local 'characters' Mum had recently been discussing with a lady in the butcher's. They included the man that sat outside the deli who'd sewn himself into his own clothes and been set alight by his German girlfriend. Then there was 'the mad Edwardian postman' who hared around on his bicycle in black tracksuit trousers with red stripes down the sides, blue satchel over his shoulder. Mum had been too embarrassed to confess her relationship to this particular 'character'.

Dad hadn't seen me and I didn't want to intrude on his drama, so I carried on up the road. When I returned there were several pairs of shoes lined on the bench next to the tramp who was swearing and cursing at them. I told Dad.

'Oh dear! His were full of holes. The weather's been so terrible, and I had a few spare pairs.'

* * *

A number of changes, both major and minor, accompanied the start of my final year at Oxford. Classicists and Linguists, both on four-year courses, were left to restructure their lives in the wake of the departure of the rest of their contemporaries. I left Cowley Road, along with Graham, who'd taken the previous year out, for a house in Summertown in the north of the city. It was cosy and comfortable, a marked improvement. I'd been invited there by two lawyers who probably would have liked to inherit the mantle of the Table Six Crew, although the table itself had been closed down after one of the Master's guests was struck by a mince pie.

Minty was living in Hammersmith, on the wrong side of the Shepherd's Bush roundabout. I disliked her house and specifically her room. One wall had been painted sky blue with a crude yellow sun; the other, black with silver moon and stars, seemed more accurately to reflect the former occupant's psychopathic disposition. He was reputed to have enjoyed starting fights in some of the dodgier local Irish pubs. Bricks had been thrown through the window of the bedroom, which retained a distinctly sinister atmosphere. Even walking to Minty's down the main Shepherd's Bush Road was hazardous, where the best way to avoid bumping into someone, at any time of day or night, was to head straight for them, since most seemed too drunk to be able to walk in a straight line.

On alternate weekends she'd come to Oxford, although our separation provided yet more fuel for a mind that writhed with the torment of my imagined infidelities. One evening, having again confronted me with unfounded accusations, Minty jumped off the bus and raced home ahead of me. I found her ripping up the photographs of herself pinned on my wall; I was too late to save the letters, fragments of which mosaiced the floor. There was one deceptively serene picture I treasured above the rest, that had been taken on a particularly happy holiday in Dorset. In it she was wearing coconut earrings in the shape of Africa I'd bought for her at Notting Hill Carnival, at a time when our fragile love had not yet suffered the fractures of suspicion. I rugby-tackled her just as she was reaching it, and pinned her to the floor.

'You're not going to have that one!'

She looked up at me, almost as tranquil as she appeared in the photograph.

'Anyway, I've done something I've wanted to do for a long time.'

There was an almost psychopathic calm to her voice.

'I've torn up the letter from that bitch!'

The one from my divorcee, my first fan letter.

'Now let me go!'

I pinned her shoulders to the floor, angry about the letters, but now concerned she shouldn't destroy the photo, which in my mind had become the sole surviving symbol of our relationship.

'Let me go, or I'll nut you!'

Like 'fuck', the word sounded so ludicrous on her lips, and with that accent that I couldn't help smiling. As I did so, she brought her head forward and butted me between the eyes. It hurt, but it amused me more, and soon we were rolling on the floor, laughing. I grabbed her and kissed her hard, my hands sliding up her legs. This sex was on a new level, more intense than ever, but though physically satisfying it no longer had any tenderness.

* * *

I began to focus all my energies on obtaining a place at music college. The natural progression would have been to study in London. My singing teacher, John Dalby, was himself a student of Eric Verthier, an eccentric Australian rumoured to conduct lessons wearing stockings and suspenders beneath his tartan trousers. John was keen for me to work with Verthier, so I applied to Trinity, the college where he taught, and was accepted. The Guildhall turned me down flat after a disastrous audition for which I arrived late and out of breath after becoming lost in the labyrinthine Barbican Centre, only to be stalked in the warm-up room by a mezzo rehearsing an aria from *Carmen*. By the time I came to face the panel I was a panting wreck. Meanwhile

Sir Geoffrey Arthur, the Master of Pembroke, was friendly with Thomas Helmsley, a well-known singer who taught at the Royal Northern College of Music in Manchester, whose vocal department had an outstanding reputation. Having heard me sing, Helmsley suggested I audition there. The contrast with my audition in London couldn't have been greater. At ease and relaxed after a full half hour's solitary preparation, I faced a panel who sat and smiled as I went through my pieces. After I'd made a complete botch of my sight-singing they simply laughed and said never mind, and they'd like to offer me a place anyway.

Although it would be a hell of a wrench to leave the South where my girlfriend, family, and most of my friends lived, from a professional point of view the RNCM was a better option than Trinity. Besides, the red blood of a United fan flowed in my veins. Living in Manchester I need never miss a game.

I also felt sad to be leaving Oxford, though I felt it was a place where most were and should be transient. By the end of my course, if nothing else, I'd mastered the art of punting. Four years ago I'd been unable to move at more than a yard a minute, or maintain a straight line for longer than two, practically dislocating my arms from their sockets each time I extricated the pole from the globigerinerooze. A hazard for other punters, source of amusement to the passengers I avenged myself on by showering with drips from the pole, I had been the anti-gondolier. Now I glided with assurance through the narrowest of gaps between floundering punts steered by the newer maladroit, past Christ Church meadow where Oxford's real hard men, the swans, molested picnicking lovers. I'd graduated to the upper reaches of the river beyond the runners, and Parson's Pleasure where naked men stood on the side of the bank displaying themselves willy nilly, to sniggering punters who were forced to slow by the depth of the water, volens nolens. At the Cherwell Boathouse Pimms and coffee cake tasted so much better with salt running into the corners of my mouth. But now the waters would no longer reflect my image.

* * *

'. . . and over the long vacation it is my belief that he should read the texts!'

Godfrey's Isaiah-like utterances began to ring in my ears once more. In concentrating my energies on life beyond Oxford, I'd failed fully to heed them. 'He could well come down in Finals!'

On balance the papers had been fair to me. But the allocation of classes for Greats at that time operated in peculiar fashion. We took ten papers, but excellence or mediocrity in any one of six of these could gain you a First or a Third, i.e. as long as you had straight Seconds in the rest, a First Class paper in Moral Philosophy would gain you a First Class degree, a Third Class one the reverse. So when I was summoned for the viva offered all borderline cases, I was delighted to find I was facing Michael Winterbottom, Godfrey Bond's star pupil. If it had been a borderline Third I felt I should have been sitting opposite one of the philosophy dons. Although Latin literature had never inspired me as much as its Greek forerunner, I still felt it was something I was good at. Besides, I had a trump card. Jo, my youngest sister, had just secured a place to study Classics at Worcester with

Winterbottom, and he'd been particularly impressed by an essay she'd written on Latin love poetry. She'd debriefed me on the answers she'd given so, when a question on this topic came up in Finals, I had been delighted.

Winterbottom glared as I sat down. He seemed unsure whether to look with greater derision at me or at the paper he had in front of him.

'Mr Glanville, you say Ovid's poetry deals with situations that are equally as real as Catullus's but you fail to prove that. In fact, I would go so far as to say that everything you write thereafter would indicate that you do not feel that to be the case.'

The roots of my hair became hedgehog prickles. This was supposed to be my star question. I'd fed all the knowledge I'd gleaned from my sister into it, designing my answer in full awareness that he, Winterbottom, would be marking it. I could only imagine that my real beliefs had come through to undermine the argument I'd constructed to impress him.

'The sensuality of Amores 1.5, where he talks about sleeping with his mistress mid-afternoon, would indicate that he's describing a real situation,' I lied.

'Yes, yes, yes, but in that case you're not answering the question, which is how far is it fair to contrast Catullus's immediacy with Ovid's unreality.'

'Well, I think it does have immediacy.' I didn't. 'But it depends on whether you're talking about the immediacy of situation or emotion.'

'I'm perfectly aware of that! Perhaps you should have begun by defining your terms . . .' He seemed furious with me. Some of the other dons began to snigger, one even interrupting to take my side, but I was already hoist with the petard of my intellectual dishonesty.

By the time the results were announced I was back in London. Someone called to tell me I had a Second, which satisfied me after the debacle of the Viva I guessed had robbed me of a First. Then I received a phone call from Geoff Sweet.

'Marco, I'm so terribly sorry.'

'Why?'

'Well, you heard, I presume.

'Yeah. I got a Second. That's fine.'

'You got a Third.'

VARIATION THREE

The Opera Singer

VARIATION THREE — *The Opera Singer*

. . . the unnameable material reality of your body,
not the one hidden by masks and disguises in the
daily ritual farce, projection of a false image aimed
at the gallery, inopportune guest who usurps your
voice and reduces it to the intermittent burbling of a
ventriloquist, but the other one, that within hours, days,
weeks, dumbfounded, bent, on its knees, defenceless as
a foetus, will repeat the gestures and mannerisms of the
suckling baby, deep-feeding, polymorph of the distant
maternal cloister, silent, proscribed truth, deprived of
the power of speech, the alter ego whisked out of the
sight of those around and of themselves by those who
aspire to the tinsel of fame

Juan Goytisolo, *Coto Vedado*

I knew I'd never need the references some of my tutors kindly
offered as a complement to my awful degree. It was unfair
(out of the ten papers Latin Literature was the only one in
which I'd received a Third) but in the world I was about to
enter it was irrelevant, and blinkered by musical ambition, I
couldn't foresee a time it might be otherwise. Friends who'd
gone into accademia, journalism, advertising and banking might
have despaired, but I was dancing with the muses, blessed by
the prospect of a life in the arts.

Manchester was bleak though. Great expanses of unlandscaped

nothingness yawned around looming tower blocks, and through it all the wind gusted, gathering cans, crisp packets, carrier bags and condoms, spraying passers-by and detritus alike with drizzle and dust. I hadn't noticed it in my time with the Cockney Reds, when its soulless expanses formed the perfect backdrop for conscienceless violence.

'Wanna watch round yerself 'ere, pal!' warned the cab driver as we left the concrete desolation of Hume and Moss Side for the stained gentility of Whalley Range and Hartley Hall, once refuge of Methodists, now residence for students at the Royal Northern College of Music.

It might have come from the cheap polish used to make the blue linoleum hallway look and feel like an ice-rink, or maybe from the crotches of a hundred and fifty over-sexed undergraduates. An oppressive, pungent odour stuck in your nostrils the moment you entered Hartley Hall. It permeated the common room, infected the chapel and seeped under the doors. And the incumbents had laid on a welcome to match. A short, thickset bloke with a bushy, bronze moustache leapt onto an improvised platform to address the hall packed with eager new arrivals unaware they were being eyed by lecherous second-year Lotharios. Later I realised there were youthful Mrs Robinsons in their midst.

'Hi everyone!' he grinned. 'My name's Pius, I'm your student union president. I'd like to welcome all of you, especially the freshers, but I don't wanna waste your time. We've got very special guests here tonight, they're the best band in Blackpool. My lords, ladies and gentlemen, a warm round of applause for the Smegma Brothers!'

On walked a bunch of Seventies refugees wearing flowery waistcoats and rockstar hair.

'Any of these studying at the college?' I asked a bloke behind me.

'You see that guy in the caftan?' came the reply from somewhere the other side of the Severn Bridge. 'The one carrying a bell? Well 'e's meant to 'ave one of the best voices in college, but I can't say, 'cos I've never 'eard 'im myself.'

He also had the longest beard and the most outrageous head-dress, a linen scarf wrapped round his head like an Arab burnous. A little acid rock, during which 'one of the best voices in college' intoned cavernously into a microphone, was followed by rather more upbeat if no less peculiar material about the joys of sniffing girls' bicycle saddles that included the Petrarchan line 'Come out of the closet and join the brotherhood. You can get yourself Aids, it'll do you good!'

'Who does he study with?'

'Paddy.'

My future teacher. I wondered how he fitted into all this, and whether I too mightn't end up on stage singing obscenities and ringing a bell.

'You a singer, yourself, then? . . . Baritone? I probably won't be talkin' to you after today.'

He invited me to the Princess, a vast pub fifteen minutes' walk away in Moss Side. Cars wormed slowly past Alexandra Park, cruising business-like girls in mini-skirts.

'Wanna watch yourself round 'ere!'

It was the second warning. My companion bought a round, and led me up some steps to a self-contained area where his friends were assembled at a couple of tables.

'Aaaah!' he called.

'Aaaah!' responded the chorus, raising their glasses.

'Got one of Paddy's 'ere. What's your name, lad?'

'Mark.'

'Welcome to the mad world of the Vocal Studies department, Mark. Aaaah!'

'Aaaah!'

They clanked their glasses, sending spume flying over chairs and tables. I lost half my pint and soon finished the remainder.

''Ere lads! A drinker! Aaaah!'

'Aaaah!'

'Aaaah!' I replied.

'Shagged anyone yet?' asked the Welshman.

'Only been 'ere five minutes!'

'Oh, I'd 'ad three already by then!'

'Anyway, I've got a girlfriend.'

'That doesn't matter!' exclaimed a tall, lean red head. 'You can 'ave mine if you want!'

A small blonde girl confirmed his offer with a laugh like a Rossini cadenza.

'Yes. You can 'ave me too if you like!'

Pius had gone to a lot of trouble. Besides the Smegma Brothers and the 'Get to know the freshers' disco with its full biblical implications, he had laid on a video of the recent college production of *The Magic Flute*, which gave me an idea of the ocean I had to cross before reaching America. I was incapable of distinguishing between the level of singing and performance in the college production, and anything I'd heard at the Royal Opera House. It was at once horrifying and thrilling.

At my first lesson Paddy was blunt.

'From what I've heard, you're not going to do it in under

four years. Your musicality is way ahead of your vocal ability. You've been singing repertoire that you oughtn't to be touching and it's set you back. Don't worry, we'll get it right between us!' he grinned, obviously registering my dismay mainly induced by the prospect of having to spend twice as long as I'd signed up for in a city I'd already written off as uninhabitable.

After a few weeks of 'Lay, lay, lahs', and the excitement of being in a place where you could talk endlessly about voice and singers without being considered a bore, I felt my voice had already improved a thousandfold, but something began to concern me. At Oxford my approach to singing had been focused on communicating the emotional intent of a song, and my voice had always dragged behind, reaching top notes or sustaining long phrases simply because it had to. This was Paddy's principal explanation for why I was in such vocal trouble. Now, I had to acquire a marketable voice and its attendant technique. That meant concentrating on developing the instrument through exercises, but the benefits of Paddy's approach were so exciting and immediate, that I began responding to the sound I was making, rather than the music and words. As a consequence the act of singing realised a different kind of fulfilment, but although it was physically exciting it was spiritually less rewarding. In spite of Paddy's delight at my progress, I now began to perceive myself more as a craftsman than an artist.

Paddy decided I'd made enough progress in the first few weeks to be entered for the late scholarship auditions. A tiny pianist flitted regularly past my door through the corridors of Hartley Hall in a black mini-dress, her hair the shape and colour of flame. I asked her whether she'd play for me. She did, and with the desired result, but our celebrations afterwards went further than I'd intended. I quickly found myself pinned to the bed with a mouthful of hairspray and her fingers moving over my crotch as deftly as they recently had the keyboard. I'd finally given Minty the grounds for her incessant accusations. My one night stand, which might have been excused as a moment of weakness soon became a casual fling that took an unwelcome turn. Each night when I returned to my room she'd be sitting outside it, her stockinged legs protruding from my door, like the Wicked Witch of the East's.

The steam valve, for those who could find it, took the form of *The English Martyrs*, an Irish Catholic drinking club. My status as a loyal Red put me on equal footing with other members there, and the club became a regular haven where I could endure Bingo nights and enjoy folk bands. I told them my Grandad was from Dublin, omitting that his family had probably arrived there by way of Lublin. The club was functional; pre-fab, strip-lit, with only a small plaque to alert passersby to its existence.

Escaping there one evening, desperate for a glimmer of sanity to lighten my nightly showdowns with the pianist, I was greeted by an unmistakable, booming St Helen's bass.

'Kiddo!'

Much to my irritation, Bob the dustman, one of the singers on my course, had found my retreat.

'Get thyself and myself a pint of ale!'

He was a fearsome figure with his dark crew-cut, blue-tinted glasses, purple blazer, black shirt, and blue and red paisley tie fastened with a tiny silver crucifix pin. Rumour had it that when everyone else was singing Verdi and Mozart he had offered 'The Cobbler's Song' from *Choo Chin Chow* at his Opera audition. I asked him.

'That's reet, kiddo! *Oh I cobble all night, and I cobble all day . . .*'

My initial embarrassment receded in the presence of one of the biggest and most beautiful voices I had ever heard. The Martyrs fell silent. Bob sat there, tone pouring forth without any visible effort, his coarse features transformed by a beatific smile, as if he were possessed by some voice demon.

I cried 'Bravo!' and the club broke into spontaneous applause.

'Bob, I had no idea. Your voice is just wonderful!'

I was shivering as I spoke, close to tears.

'The head of Vocal Studies said to me when I sang at my audition, "Where've you been all these years? We've been waiting for you!" But I'll tell you what, kiddo, you don't know what life's about till you've 'ad two 'undred weight of ash on each shoulder!'

He lit up a heavy-tarred fag and downed most of his pint in one.

'God!' I exclaimed, shocked to see someone drinking even faster than me.

'That's reet, kiddo! He cares for you as he cares for me!'

A middle-aged blonde woman shuffled past and picked up the ashtray. Bob rested his hand on the back of hers with a little too much intimacy.

''Old on, Sheila! Ah in't finished yet!'

He placed her hand on the table, flicked the ash from his fag, and grinned with an innuendo inappropriate to his crucifix tie-pin. After what I'd seen of Christians at Oxford, I shouldn't have been surprised.

'I'm not in a hurry to get back tonight.'

'Oh aye. An' why's that, kiddo?'

'I'm being stalked.'

'What's thou mean?'

'There's this girl who sits outside my door every night.'

'Ah shouldn't complain.'

'Yeah, but I'm not interested.'

'Ah 'ad a bit of a problem recently. Bloke ah'd bin playin' cards wit'. Found out 'e'd marked the deck!'

'That's bad.'

'Bad! That were only t' beginning. Next thing, 'e's wakin' me 'ole fam'ly, bangin' on knocker at two in t' mornin'! Kept 'appenin' till one of the neighbours saw 'im. So 'e starts doin' same wit' me Gran!'

'What do you mean?'

'Knockin' on 'er door all times o' night. So I tracked 'im down. "YOU!" I said. "YOU!" Shoulda seen 'is face!'

I could. He'd virtually sent me into orbit with the force of his exclamations.

'"Ah've gorra bone ter pick wit' yer! FIRST! You've bin cheatin' at cards. SECOND! You've been playin' knockie doors wit' me fam'ly. THIRD! And worst of all. You've bin TERRORISIN' ME GRANNY!'

'Did you whack him?'

'Didn'ave ter!'

I asked him whether he had any other numbers up his sleeve. Without drawing breath he launched into *Old Man River*, signature tune of his vocal ancestor Paul Robeson. He started very low, rolling out bottom notes normally only reached by Slavonic choirs, but lost the plot a bit halfway through and was nearing the finish in a far higher key. I wondered if such a low voice could possibly hit the notes it was heading for. But he soared to a series of top B flats that would have flattered Pavarotti, again without any apparent effort. I'm sure he'd never studied voice seriously or thought about how he produced these amazing sounds. His vocal apparatus operated flawlessly, its technical perfection a gift of nature. Most singers spent years studying for it but seldom achieved it. It was as if Bob's voice existed in a different dimension, and while he sang he was in harmony with the celestial spheres.

It was past midnight when I returned, just six hours before the tower clock's chimes would once again knock nails through the dreams of sleeping musicians, in cruel reminder of the nine-to-five world they thought their talent had allowed them to escape. She was still there; tiny and forlorn in my doorway, eyeliner heavy against her pallid skin, and amber hair standing as if in shock at her.

'Annie, what do you want?'

She gave me the mournful, knowing look my rhetorical question merited.

'Annie, please let me go to bed. I'm tired.'

I opened my door and she followed me in.

'Minty's coming up this weekend. I don't want it to go on. Please go.'

'I won't be around when she's here. I'll disappear.'

'Fine. But I mean now, ever. I want this to end.'

She pulled her thin black cotton dress over her head, removed her tights, then her underwear and climbed into my bed.

'Annie, please get out of my bed and put your clothes back on.'

She rolled over and faced the wall.

'Okay, I'm going out, and when I come back I want you gone.'

It wasn't the most forceful ultimatum.

Down the corridor, past two sets of fire doors, the faint aroma of ganja signalled that Dave the guitarist was up. I knocked.

'Wha'!'

The door cracked open, leaving a gap just large enough for his blonde moustache.

'Oh, it's you! You can't smell anything out there, can you?'

'It's like a fucking reggae club at closing time!'

'Oh wha'! Shit!'

He staggered about the room, gathering up various items of clothing, which he stuffed against the foot of the door before proffering me an immaculately rolled spliff.

'Bad for the voice.'

'You singers are all the same. Bunch of fucking nancies!'

I described my predicament, and he went into paroxysms of drug-fuelled laughter, tears falling down his face. After a while he was obviously getting off on the sheer sensation of mirth, its cause long forgotten. I began to laugh myself, but after five minutes I landed, and experienced the cold turkey of the situation I still had to deal with.

'Look, I've got an unwanted naked girl in my bed . . .'

'Ha haaaah!'

His guffaws followed me outside, leaving me to face reality. To my surprise the bed was empty, but I couldn't sleep and so I went back to Dave's room. Returning half an hour later, I was relieved that her telltale legs weren't there to greet me, but the door, which in a semi-stoned mixture of anxiety and euphoria I'd forgotten to lock, was open, and the duvet, ominously, proud of the bed. She seemed to be asleep. Too tired to go through the sturm and drang of kicking her out I climbed in beside her. Within seconds she was pushing herself against my back and reaching between my legs, but she felt oily and gritty as she climbed on top of me. *Ven der putz steht* . . .

After it was over, my hair was full of it, my body covered in it.

'When you were gone I took your dressing-gown and went outside. It felt great, just rolling and rolling in the mud.'

When the clock chimed at six I saw I had a problem. The mud was everywhere – the sheets, the pillow, the duvet. My bedding wouldn't be changed until the following week, and Minty was arriving in a few days. The real explanation was so implausible that the one I gave her, that I'd been playing football and had been too tired to have a shower before climbing into bed, sounded reasonable by comparison.

She arrived on the weekend of the Manchester derby, noticed the dirty sheets but accepted my lies with a chuckle and a reprimand. At the back of the Stretford End, where I'd bought two seats as a concession to her first-ever visit to a football match, the passionate bustle of fans excited by the prospect of stuffing detested City simply irritated her. When Stapleton pulled one back for United and we leapt from our uncomfortable metal seats to share our joy with strangers, Minty remained in hers and glared, a still figure amidst the fervent celebrants.

'I don't like being grabbed. First you did, then some horrid oaf who's practically sitting on my knee.'

So when Stapleton hit his second to level the score at 2–2, I hugged the bloke next to me instead. If a United v City match couldn't move her nothing would. It occurred to me she hadn't known me when I was fanatically following the Reds all over the country. It was a pastime that had gone on hold at Oxford but would be easier than ever to pursue now. The vast crowd dispersed. We passed through the depopulated council estates of Moss Side and Hulme.

'Next time I come, make sure there isn't another dreadful football match.'

'That's as good as you'll get.'

'Exactly!'

Yet despite all our differences and the terminal decline of our relationship, against the sullen background of Manchester Minty still sparkled with the charm of a life in Oxford and London I'd left behind. It was a life I felt I had to distance myself from if I were to survive in the new environment. I was so convinced the Royal Northern would furnish me with the key I needed to enter the singing profession, that I was prepared to adapt and reinvent myself if I had to. So I tried not to spend too much time in London during the interminable terms that sprawled across the year like fat women on a beach, aimless and lethargic, devoid of Michaelmas, Hilary and Trinity's intense passion.

After Minty went I decided to put an end to any further

contact with Annie who'd begun to sit vigil outside my room again the very evening Minty had returned to London. She hammered and cried for twenty minutes before finally leaving. At three in the morning I awoke from a recurring nightmare of cowering in the bushes to escape a ferocious Vietnamese air and land assault. 'B-lat! B-lat!' They were closer than usual, but then I realised that these sounds were real. My door was being attacked. I shouted at the dream creature who, in my half-waking state, had become imbued with the temper and stature of an ogress. But that only inspired her to greater ferocity. I had to press my shoulder against the door to stop it giving way to her running kicks. After a good half hour she tired and left, but a little after that I heard a scream and a loud crack. Having failed with me she'd tried to storm the bedroom of another victim and he'd knocked her unconscious. Her nightly visitations ceased, but the dearth of available women at Oxford was matched by the shortage of straight men at the Royal Northern, and before the first term was out I'd been unfaithful with two other girls. They were soulless encounters that reflected the deadening of my own emotions.

*

The backdrop of windswept Troy was no less stark. It was the setting for Edward Bond's suitably bleak play *The Woman*, in which I had my first solo performing opportunity. Each year the second-year Vocal Studies students were expected to put on a full scale theatrical production, and as there were so few men in the year above me, those of us on the performing course in my year were asked to make up numbers. I'd been assigned the role of the Greek high priest, Bob was my chaplain, and I had an assistant priest in the shape of a cheerful young baritone called Peter who occasionally joined me in the chorus on the United Road.

As I passed through the refectory before the first rehearsal, Bob summoned me.

'Kiddo! Get thyself and myself a cup of tea!'

Most of the singers sat in the non-smoking coffee shop through which various hostile brass players passed, puffing defiantly, but I was happier away from their endless conversations about sex and singing. At first they'd been refreshing; now they made me yearn for the monastic quads I'd left behind.

'Have you learnt your lines yet?' he inquired, lighting up a fag.

'Not hard. Have you?'

'The goddess speaks Greek in the spiritual sense.'

'The goddess speaks Greek in the spiritual sense.'

'The Greek eternity speaking to the Greek temporality.'

'The Greek eternity speaking to the Greek temporality.'

'Bless you brother . . .'

'Bless you brother . . .'

'Bob! That's the one you don't repeat!'

'Sorry, kid!'

Malcolm the director was in the theatre where rehearsals were already in progress, his eyes alight behind round, metal-rimmed glasses. He always looked as if he were about to burst out laughing.

'OK, chaps! How are we? Learned our lines yet?'

The two second-year men went through their heated dialogue. I heard my cue and burst in.

'Too late!'

We returned, remorsefully, to our original positions. I began to feel self-conscious.

'Now you've just seen a couple of Trojan priests, your hated rivals, leaving the commander's tent. You're absolutely livid.'

I stormed on again, trying to appear furious, but the feeling had gone into my legs, making my movements disjointed and comic rather than dramatic. Behind me came Bob in his tinted glasses and evangelical tiepin, followed by handsome, shock-headed Peter.

'*Sir, there was no doubt!*' I exploded. For some reason it sounded exactly like Windsor Davies' buffo sergeant in *It Ain't 'Alf 'Ot Mum*. Hero and Nestor burst into loud guffaws.

'It's like the Marx brothers coming on stage!'

Twenty minutes later the laughter had receded, but the director had an impish streak. Rather than bringing out the drama, he made the scene increasingly comic, the priests endlessly circling the officers who didn't know which way to turn to address us. We finally convinced ourselves that Edward Bond had intended us as the comic relief in an otherwise unremittingly gloomy play. My problem was solved. If the walk looked ridiculous it was acceptable. I conveniently forgot that it was my self-consciousness and lack of technique that had made it look strange in the first place.

Now I only had to pass the test of the dress rehearsal, but as I came off stage after the first act, someone who'd been watching it for the first time, and wasn't to be fooled, descended.

'Mark! Come over here!' she snapped. 'What on earth do you think you're doing. It's all going perfectly, and suddenly you come on and it's like something straight out of *The Black and White Minstrel Show!*'

'Yes!' chimed in Malcolm. 'What were you doing? You've never played it like that before.'

Summoned to her room for a one-to-one session, I assumed she'd attempt to darken the lightness I'd brought to the play. I admitted to having found the key to my character in Windsor Davies' sergeant, and suggested my ability as a mimic should help my acting.

'It's your imitating that gets in your way, lovey.'

Elaine was joint Head of Diction and Movement. Reputedly able to lip-read, she seemed equally adept at reading minds. A latterday sibyl, she helped those less happy with their own multi-dimensionality. It was the ones who never felt the need to question what or who they were that were most successful on stage. They instinctively drew on elements within themselves, without reaching, as I did, for something beyond.

'Heel, ball, toe. Heel, ball, toe. You have a tendency to bounce when you walk. Quite a common fault, lovey. It's conditioning.'

And I knew whose. Nanny Jeanette. 'You're not walking properly!' WHACK. 'You're not walking properly!' THUMP. Even strolling down the high street now I'd suddenly become very conscious of what my feet were doing, so the attentions of opera directors and movement specialists were almost unendurable. Their scrutiny made me feel desperately self-conscious and tense. Without a neutral position I lacked the simple root of truth from which the relevant emotional gesture might branch. I wondered whether Nanny Jeanette might not also be the reason why I avoided looking people in the face in a public place, afraid they might detect some nameless guilt or crime. So I instinctively fought Elaine, chiefly because she'd become a nanny surrogate, but also because I understood that she was trying to strip my defences, and I knew the uncomfortable, raw vulnerability she engendered in me was an emanation from what lay buried beneath the jungle. I realised I had no idea which of the masks I inhabited were mine. None seemed to supply the neutrality required to act. I'd long presented a number of masks to a world that had no interest in checking their validity as long as it could negotiate with them.

Just as a hermit crab acquires the discarded shells of other molluscs in order to protect its soft, vulnerable body, so I felt I'd had no choice but to don the mask of lads and hooligans. At first it had seemed the only way to survive at a tough inner-city comprehensive, but I'd worn it so long that even I had forgotten what really was beneath it, what I had originally been, and, at heart, still was. Although I now needed to discard the shell in order to successfully realise the stage roles I hoped would be thrown at me; paradoxically, the environment and conditions I'd found in Manchester were better suited to the shell than its guest.

These difficulties were accentuated by the direction my vocal development was taking. I'd arrived at the Royal Northern as a baritone but had been trained as a bass ever since. In opera my dark, lyric voice type was best suited to the portrayal of old men, rather than the villains and seducers who were far more fun to play and closer to my age and temperament. As a *basso cantante* I was trapped playing aged fathers and ancient priests, trying to imagine what it was like to be forty years older, struggling to reconcile what I was with what I was expected to portray. Although Elaine was right to criticise me, the repertoire I was assigned meant it was easier to replicate the mannerisms of others rather than search within for emotions and experiences to simulate those of much older men. It was very difficult to sing and perform with the emotional honesty that audiences instinctively appreciate.

In the meantime my sound was becoming more 'impressive' and therefore marketable. At the Royal Northern big voices were highly regarded by staff and students, which was realistic, since that's what a three-thousand-seater opera house would require. The problem was that they were admired in much the same way as big cocks. Sometimes I struggled to recall that it was the transcendent quality of Schubert and Verdi which had led me to Manchester, and the belief that interpreting their music would bring the double catharsis of expressing myself and satisfying an audience.

At least I didn't have to worry about such niceties at Old Trafford. I reckoned that if I sang my head off there on Saturday afternoon, my vocal cords would be recovered in time for my singing lesson on Tuesday. Fifteen minutes from Maine Road, twenty from Old Trafford, the Royal Northern was ideally situated for anyone with an interest in football, though few seemed inclined to take advantage. I went to all United's home games and as many aways as I could in the company of Dave the guitarist, forsaking the Scoreboard Paddock of my youth for the United Road End on the opposite touchline. Many former colleagues had switched allegiance since they'd moved the visiting supporters to the adjacent enclosure. At times, especially when the likes of Everton and

Liverpool were playing, we felt like a lone outpost in the face of hugely superior numbers.

'Come a come a come a come a come a United Road' we'd challenge them, to the tune of Culture Club's *Karma Chameleon* (on one occasion West Ham's Inter City Firm did and nearly had a result). The freedom and exhilaration of singing 'Glory, glory Man United' on United Road made up for the mundane tedium of day-to-day existence at the Royal Northern.

I got out of Hartley Hall as quickly as I could, and found a flat in Chorlton with Dave, twenty minutes' walk from Mecca. We'd stroll up Seymour Grove for League and Cup games, friendlies, reserve and youth team matches where you could spot future stars. It was a United fanatic's dream, and it would almost have been impossible to better that first season, which ended in two Cup finals. Once I took along a Welsh tenor. Unable to resist the allure of singing 'Man United, Man United, we'll support you ever more', to the tune of *Bread of Heaven* in an excruciatingly high football crowd key, he belted the whole thing out in his resonant voice, sounding unsettlingly civilised amongst the raucous hordes. Unlike me, he left the ground with his voice intact.

At Arsenal, pre-match entertainment had always been supplied by the singing policeman. At Old Trafford we had Smiler, named for the satisfied grin he wore at all times. Smiler seemed to be in charge of our area of the ground. It was where most of the troublemakers were concentrated, and he'd acquired grudging respect for the fearless way he hauled offenders out of the ground, after various warnings, in the form of a raised eyebrow or glint. However big the thug, however many mates, nothing would save him from Smiler. Once his job was done he'd return to the touchline and smile at us again, always obliging when we sang 'Smiler, Smiler give us a wave!' with a classic Dixon of Dock Green salute.

With the exception of local rivals or Cup games, only Chelsea brought large numbers. At such times we'd stand on the corner of Chester Road and exchange insults and missiles, but, apart from when we knocked Everton out of the Cup, the police had the situation under control. On that occasion Shockheaded Peter nearly lost his hand after a shopkeeper caught it in the door he was slamming in the face of rampaging scousers. I was standing on the pavement, watching Everton fans attack people and property, feeling calm in a protective bubble of euphoria conjured by the approaching prospect of an F.A. Cup semi-final.

But I had a much closer shave at Luton, turning into a side-street leading to an alleyway by the visiting supporters' end. A United firm I'd never seen before was turning over vegetable stalls outside an Asian cornershop when a smaller Luton crew attacked them. It was a grave misjudgement. One was caught and held spread-eagled while they took it in turn to kick his swinging head. When I emerged at the other side of the alleyway and found a United fan nursing a lip split like a fig, I was grateful for their intervention. It would have been me next.

I had never liked Spurs, ever since they wrecked my first visit to Old Trafford. I had fought them on the Loftus Road terraces with QPR supporters and at White Hart Lane with United. Their north London location has given them a large Jewish following, no bigger than Arsenal's, but for some reason it was Spurs who acquired the nickname 'Yids', even if most of those who revel in it would have had nothing to fear in Hitler's Germany. To those who abuse Spurs fans as 'Yids' the word is generally no more than a label, though it can be hard to distinguish anti-Semitism from the hard-edged mockery that constitutes part of a football hooligan's armoury and leads to chants about the 1958 Munich air crash in which most of United's glamorous young side was wiped out, and gloating over rival fans' deaths.

We were at home. As usual I stood as close as I could to the opposition supporters, under Smiler's attentive gaze. A tall crew-cut bloke in grey trench-coat pushed his way to the front and began chanting abuse:

> 'Spurs are on their way to Auschwitz
> Hitler's gonna gas 'em again.
> Who's gonna gas 'em?
> We're gonna gas 'em
> The Yids from White Hart Lane'

a number that comes complete with hissing noises. Others in his extensive anti-Semitic repertoire I'd not heard before, and there were even a few old Mosleyite numbers:
'The Yids, the Yids, we gotta get rid of the Yids!'
I knew all the faces on the United Road, and I'd certainly have taken note of his. It was his first appearance there. None of the regulars followed his lead, but that didn't deter him.

Smiler was watching, so I waited for my moment, unable to concentrate on the game, keeping my blood pressure high by focussing my fury on the head of the fascist, who himself hadn't displayed the least interest in events on the pitch. As we left the ground I kept him in my sights, pushing through the crowd until I was in the tunnel behind him. I wasn't interested in a fair fight. I stopped to create space for myself and karate-kicked him in the small of the back with as much force as I could muster. He spun round, rubbing his spine. I stared straight at him, wondering how often he'd revelled in others' fear, but, disappointingly, he looked past me, turned and walked on. Bang! I caught him again. Bang! and again. It was a while since I'd struck someone in anger and I'd forgotten how good it felt. He started to move faster, breaking into a jog as we left the tunnel, and didn't appear at the next home game or ever again.

* * *

Though I couldn't wait to return to London each time another Royal Northern term rolled lethargically into the station, I was keener to keep up with my other Oxford friends than with Minty. The distance between London and Manchester reflected the one between us. No one else was involved: all my relationships at college were as barren of sentiment as other facets of my life there. I called her from the kitchen in my Chorlton flat to tell her it was over. It meant I didn't have to offer a traitor's consoling arm or cope with the reality of what it meant to her. I could put whatever interpretation I liked on her sobbing, the knee-jerk reaction to the death of something long in decay.

Like the boy in the story of the Snow Queen, after shards of the devil's shattered mirror had entered his eye and heart, distorting his vision and freezing his emotions, I was incapable of seeing or feeling the callousness of my actions. It was a paradox. I was pursuing a career in an art form I'd once considered to be the successful synthesis of all other arts, but rather than building on what I'd discovered towards the end of my time at Oxford, my Manchester experience had eroded that edifice. Whether it was the pragmatism of a city beset by poverty and lousy weather, or the nature of a profession more trade than art form, love felt out of place. Yet, where Bob the Dustman could surprise me with the angel of his voice, there was always hope that something could transcend the rubbish-strewn wastes of the city. It came, deceptively clad, in the college's production of Britten's *Gloriana*.

Sadly for Bob, in the eyes of the Opera Department his lack of basic musicianship and unreliability cancelled out his undeniable vocal qualities, and they seemed to have decided that I was a better prospect. Accordingly I was cast as the Recorder of Norwich, the smallest and oldest of the three bass roles in *Gloriana*. No Windsor Davies impressions would see me through. Paddy was prepared to lift the dust-sheet off my sculpture as far as the knee on which, according to the libretto, I would have fallen had my age allowed, but 'My bones are old' apparently came out as 'My balls are old', so the work was far from complete. There was no doubt I could be heard, so one piece was in place, but otherwise I found it an endurance test, from the spirit gum that inflamed my nostrils to the long, irritating beard that it glued to my chin in a desperate attempt to add another fifty years. Elaine had me pacing her room, heavy and flat-footed; successive directors and movement specialists force-fed me the elixir of senility and in the end I just about got there.

One man made the whole thing worthwhile. I'd seen him

on the day I arrived, wearing a caftan and intoning filth
into a microphone. But it had been three years before the
conservative college was prepared to let us hear the voice
that no one had heard but everyone talked about. All he had
to do was sit and sing a four-verse ballad (it was as much as
they were prepared to risk) and I was one of several London
beggars lucky enough to be on stage when he did so. His
voice was as big a revelation as Bob's had been, except with
the clarity and focus a live performance and its attendant
rehearsals required. I couldn't understand why they were
worried. While Elizabeth, Essex and Mountjoy gallivanted
about, John Connell sat there, and through simple honesty
of utterance coupled with a sound whose beauty, power
and richness no words are adequate to describe, provided
the catharsis every music lover seeks. Standing by his side I
was aware of no extraneous movement or tension. I felt as I
heard him that what he expressed was a truth which grasped
the essence of what he was, even though at that stage I didn't
know him, a demon dark and sad, yet noble, light years from
the character who'd sung about sniffing bicycle saddles on my
first evening in Hartley Hall.

Dave introduced us. The three of us sat in the refectory one
afternoon, watching breasts and buttocks wobble down the
aisles between the tables. I told him how much his singing
had moved me.

'Ooh! I think I can feel a little movement of me own!' he
grinned, adjusting himself in his chair, much to the amusement
of Dave.

'You know I nearly didn't do it? They had me singing in
the chorus. I told them I wouldn't be able to keep me voice
anchored. I never sang anyway, then one of the ballet dancers'

hands brushed against me knob in the masque sequence.' Dave guffawed loudly.

'Hoooh! I was in agony. I've got a really tight foreskin. I couldn't carry on singing after that, with all those pert little bodies flitting about. It might happen again. I told them it was too dangerous.'

'And they let you off?'

'No. I just stopped coming.'

'What, in the rehearsal or after it?'

We sat there shaking with laughter, attracting derisory looks from passing members of staff.

'If I get really famous and rich I'm going to patent a cough medicine and call it Connell Linctus. You know, I've been told I've got the perfect face for oral sex – big nose and a bushy moustache.'

He flicked his tongue between his teeth rapidly to prove the point.

'Ah, Pippa! Come and sit on me face, I mean me knee!'

A slight, giggly blonde teenager took up the offer. Her hair tickled John's cheek and brushed against the pint glass he was holding.

'So how's life treating you, Pippa?'

'I've got a History lecture in five minutes and I've just had my violin lesson.'

'Oh! That's a shame.'

'Why's that?'

''Cos it means you won't be sitting on me knee much longer,' John snorted.

'Anyway, best be going now. Byee!'

'Byee!' mimicked John.

Pippa was oblivious to the mockery.

'Hang on a minute!'

He levered his Falstaffian frame out of the uncomfortable plastic chair, and with pint glass in one hand and camera in the other, began to waddle down the aisle behind her. Moments later he was back.

'Have a look at this.'

He produced a photo album from his bag. Inside were pictures of girls' backsides. They had all been taken clandestinely in various locations around college. I identified an ex's tight red and white striped cut-aways.

'She found out. I thought she was going to kill me!'

I flicked through the rest. There was nothing arousing about this collection of clothed, often out of focus, disembodied buttocks. I wondered how long it had taken him to work out the optimum position in which to hold the camera.

'You know Pippa? I'd like to push her head down over me cock and have her gobbling there, and then I'd come and it'd be like fucking Vesuvius, all over her hair and her head, and then in two thousand years there'll be an archaeological dig, and they'll chip away and find this girl still bent over, suckin' me knob!'

He erupted into uncontrollable laughter.

Wild as he was, John's voice had now been unveiled in all its majestic splendour. There was no way the genie could be put back in the bottle. To the chagrin of some of those who'd spent weeks perfecting the detail of their vocal and dramatic characterisations, John just turned up, sat down, sang and walked off with all the best reviews, offers of contracts and auditions with major companies. But when he turned up at Opera North, they handed him a broom and asked him to sweep the stage, so little did he conform to the stereotype of an opera singer. I never heard a more beautiful bass voice.

Its vulnerable masculinity seemed so successfully to reconcile virility and sensitivity. From that time it served as my model, since its natural perfection was something to which I would always be aspiring.

Watching John and a few others picking up principal contracts was encouraging for all of us. Being in the presence of such people coupled with the opportunity this gave us to hear fine singing at close quarters, accelerated our own development at a startling rate that would have been impossible to achieve had we been studying in a vacuum. As my larynx lowered, my throat opened and the sound became clearer, I began to enjoy my voice much more. So much so that I drove my neighbours and housemates mad with interminable exercises. And I feared colds as much as a footballer a strained hamstring.

By the following term, Paddy was happy for me to be heard as Sparafucile, the hired assassin of *Rigoletto*. I was given thigh-length leather boots, a dapper painted moustache and a long-bladed knife which I could sharpen suggestively in the pub where I was landlord. Verdi had written the role lyrically, much of it with little accompaniment, making Sparafucile a villain who requires beautiful singing, calm and insidious as he goes about his gruesome work. It meant I didn't have to impose a harsh (or 'evil') sound onto my natural voice, and I could strut about the stage as myself, except with a callous, murderous intent. We performed our potted version of *Rigoletto*, with piano accompaniment, in the opera theatre to a college audience, always the most critical. Many were only there in the hope of seeing a rival take a fall, but after the old men I finally had a character I could revel in and took a great deal of pleasure in projecting it.

My hired assassin led to a number of offers both on and off stage, the former sowing the seeds for future professional growth, the latter leading to one night stands, and various relationships that dissolved like tablets in water. As far as I was able to, I still went to every commutable United game, but my voice was now being regularly exposed to public scrutiny and required maintenance, and I could no longer be reckless with it on the terraces. The unhappy compromise involved taking my traditional tenorial pitch down an octave, which earned me pitying looks from hardcore songsters who obviously thought I'd suddenly gone tone deaf. I probably should have worried more about the possible physical damage from being a member of United's Red Army. There were a few close shaves, mainly in Liverpool, only forty miles down the road, easy to reach but perilous to leave. After running the gauntlet of a rock and bottle attack outside Stanley Park where our exit was blocked by a line of nose to tail coaches, I watched in amazement as a teenage girl emerged from behind a large Union Jack inscribed 'Munich 58' to hurl a brick through the window of our bus and into the head of the bloke sitting in front of me. Equally unforgettable was the bloodthirsty cheer that greeted a bottle smashing into the forehead of a teenage kid standing next to me. He left the Cup semi at Goodison with blood streaming through his fingers and over his clothes.

* * *

It was after chasing the scousers down Chester Road one October afternoon that I came to terms once again with Malcolm Fraser, the director who'd allowed me to get away with murder as the Greek priest. The college was putting on a major production of Debussy's *Pelleas et Melisande*, in which I was to play the role of Arkel, the half-blind ancient King of Allemonde.

'He's pretty old this character, isn't he?'

'How old d'you reckon, Malcolm?'

''Bout a hundred.'

'Thanks a lot!'

He roared with laughter. (There wasn't any in the piece.)

'Right. I think you should have attendants, so I'm giving you a group of servant girls.'

'Brilliant! Can I choose them? I think they should all be wearing black stockings and suspenders.'

It was the last light moment.

He hadn't been joking about Arkel's age. They even made up prosthetic cheeks, which were glued to my own and left them red raw when removed. What with the weight of my costume and the oppressive wig and beard, by the time I reached the stage I already felt ground down by the *Weltschmerz* from which Arkel's oracular utterances spring. Such was the exaggeration of my make-up, I need only move slowly and ponderously to persuade an audience, but I found an inner connection too. My posture and lethargy engendered feelings I'd thought were far beyond my experience. Exploring Arkel led me to discover within myself the strong paternal instinct that governs his actions, like the female egg waiting, since the very birth of the mother, to be fertilised. Everything in Arkel's world was so bleak, that inhabiting him I also became very depressed. Far removed as he was, on the surface, from my experience and milieu, he vibrated strings normally too painfully sensitive for me to touch. Arkel's music was written for a French *basse chante* and its tessitura suited my own dark but high-lying voice. In it I could explore the *vuoto* (literally 'empty') sound Paddy loved so much, whose disembodied sensation itself took me to a new spiritual level, open like the sound I felt I was producing. Recordings where Arkel's utterances were thrown away like a series of asides irritated me. To me each of his phrases had inherent weight and significance. Once I was used to the sensation of age and the claustrophobic cling of the piece, I began to experience its catharsis. Whereas Sparafucile's sinuous, thigh-boot-clad evil turned girls on, I developed an almost father-daughter relationship with the servant girls I'd joked about at our first rehearsal.

I auditioned for Glyndebourne after they'd heard me as Arkel, and was offered a chorus job. The weekend before my contract was due to begin I went to visit Graham, my old Oxford housemate who was now living in Birmingham. Fortuitously, Welsh National Opera would be performing *Otello* there on the Friday while United were down the road at Coventry the following day. Peter Stein's was a sophisticated production, in which he tried to impose the presumed conventions of a seventeenth-century Globe production onto late nineteenth-century Italian opera; I found it profoundly unmoving, and left the theatre still needing a fix.

At the end of a season that had begun with ten straight victories, United had once again rolled over for Liverpool. Nonetheless, at Coventry we strolled to a comfortable 3–1 win and a probable place in Europe. Towards the end of the game I noticed a leery-looking group of home supporters leave the ground, responding to the usual chants of 'We can see you sneaking out' by waving and blowing kisses. We'd driven down from Birmingham, and Graham had parked his car in a sidestreet above the stadium. As we made our way back there, I noticed a mob of about twenty men, clustered purposefully on a corner about twenty yards from the car, one of them a member of the group who'd blown kisses at us fifteen minutes earlier. I sensed danger. Graham continued chatting nonchalantly, oblivious of their presence, but I could almost feel the drops of the cloud about to burst. I barred his path with my arm, but he pushed it aside. I pulled him back again.

'What's the problem?'

'Those blokes.'

'Oh, for fuck's sake!'

Three United fans walked past us and into a hail of bottles, some of which smashed on the road, others against cars. A few hit their targets. It was the classic preliminary to an off. They looked shocked and confused, but this was only the beginning. Letting out a primordial roar the gang fell on them. It was like watching helpless impalas being dragged to the ground and savaged by a pride of lions. Ferocious punches and powerful kicks rained on the two who hadn't been quick enough to escape. One I lost sight of beneath a swarm that picked and plucked at him. Meanwhile his friend was shoved against Graham's car, onto which two of the gang jumped, the better to kick him in the face and head, which swung like a conker from the impact of the blows. Others laid into his body, their boots and punches delivered with maximum power, thudding into flesh, cracking against bone. Blood ran through his hair, hennaing it; swollen gashes scarred his cheeks and forehead, his nose was flattened. It probably took no more than a minute to finish two between twenty, though time had frozen for the duration of the assault. One lay unconscious on the ground while his friend, hideously disfigured, staggered about the road, fixing each of us in turn. 'Where the fuck's the Red Army now? Where's the fucking Red Army?' Graham's car also bore the scars of the assault. Muddy foot-marks stained its bodywork and one of its wings had been dented by a miscued boot.

I was relieved that I'd saved us from a similar fate, but my head felt horribly numb. Where was the Red Army? I tried to rationalise my own shameful non-involvement. We were so outnumbered that if we'd tried to save them, we'd only have become victims ourselves. Even worse than the guilt were the images that whizzed round my head all day, reappearing more vividly at night. It was the sort of beating I'd often heard described but never previously experienced or witnessed. When the horrific events were simply the details of someone else's saga, their images faded as swiftly as those of a Hammer horror film. Even the colourful language in which such stories were couched had its own lurid allure. But it was a quantum leap from the savagery of the feelings evoked in me at football matches to their active realisation. I'd never hurt or wanted to harm anybody in the way these thugs just had. It was little short of a miracle that I'd neither witnessed nor been on the end of such a hammering before. Such had been my need for the catharsis football hooliganism provided that I'd blinded myself to the truth of what might be the real end to a dangerous game I'd been playing on and off for fifteen years.

* * *

The gentle rain on the Downs slowly washed away the memory

of Coventry's blood-spattered back streets. Glyndebourne itself had been transformed. Traditionally the province of the white English upper-middle classes, its usual vanilla was chocolate chipped by the cast and chorus of *Porgy and Bess*. They roamed the protecting green of its magnificent grounds, surprising the regulars. Old ladies looked about anxiously.

'Who are all these negroes?' I heard one ask in a mixture of fear and irritation.

Some of the English members of the *Porgy* chorus doubled alongside me as courtiers and plebeians in Verdi's *Simone Boccanegra*. Their vitality failed to lift a production, which, without a single Italian principal, simply lacked the larger-than-life passion needed to send middle-period Verdi across the footlights, even if it was only Middle England waiting beyond them. *Porgy*, despite the misgivings of some patrons and a certain conductor, saved the season. The detail and intimacy of its relationships, portrayed with overwhelming intensity, came over forcefully in the small theatre.

Abraham, Harry and Lloyd, one Nigerian and the other two of Jamaican origin, all spoke as aristocratically as the dukes and earls who'd come to hear us. 'Good Lord!' they told me. 'You speak better patois than we do!' We spent a lot of time together, at first commuting on trains between Sussex and London, then clubbing at The Pink Coconut in Brighton, where Abraham turned up in a foreign legionnaire's outfit and showed us how his dancing had won him a holiday in Spain.

It was a relief to exchange the miserable grey functionalism of Manchester for the Arcadia of Glyndebourne with its views from the ha-ha across undulating green fields speckled with cotton-wool sheep. The Downs beyond seemed to harness an ancient energy, protected by the rim they formed. That summer the sun shone on the punters' picnics and on our drinking sessions, and tennis matches where Harry and I whacked Anglo-Saxon balls across the net. Besides Abraham, Harry and Lloyd, I also spent a lot of time with Sylvia, Jadey and Jane in pubs. The fizzle of sexual tension in the wire beneath the surface added excitement to our friendships, but after six years I felt as cleansed by an extended period of chastity as by the inspiring beauty of the landscape and environment in which I was working. I shared a room with a sparring partner from Manchester, and each night we laughed ourselves to sleep reminiscing about the people and events of the day.

Charles Kerry, whose voice had so impressed me as Rocco in the Oxford production of *Fidelio*, was chorus manager, and gave seafront parties with homemade kelp relish, when he wasn't telling members of the chorus to go and have their hair abbreviated. 'Why can't you just say fucking haircut like anyone else?' demanded a Royal Northern tenor. Glyndebourne's camp gentility makes it the only opera house in my experience to correspond to the average outsider's notion of what such places must be like.

Most of the carefully selected *Porgy* cast had been flown over from the States. No effete English custom could sway Gregg Baker's statuesque, ex-American footballer's six foot six inch frame. In this production, before seducing Bess, he had to rip off his shirt to reveal a perfectly sculpted torso, an act that elicited a subterranean grunt from the girl sitting next to me at the dress rehearsal. Up in the gods we sweltered tropically. When Willard White's Porgy, having lost his beloved Bess, walks into the apotheosis of an almost kitsch radiant dawn, such was the powerful realism of the performance preceding this moment, that I wept and wept, my tears so mingling with my sweat that I could almost convince people I hadn't been crying when the houselights came up. I felt as if Glyndebourne's catharsis had washed the shard of glass from the devil's mirror out of my eye, even if the one in my heart was still not completely dislodged. Everyone else seemed to have gone through something similar: one by one, the entire audience rose to its feet to give the show a standing ovation.

But while *Porgy*'s moon waxed *Simone*'s waned. So much so that the BBC pulled the plug on the broadcast and video for whose financial fruits many had signed up, the excuse being that there had been an argument over Peter Hall's refusal to relinquish full directorial control of the televisation. The story made the front page of *The Sunday Times* who'd been pursuing Hall and Nunn with allegations that they'd been making private fortunes out of publicly funded theatre, and the atmosphere at Glyndebourne turned sour as each chorister was interrogated in an attempt to uncover the mole. While Glyndebourne buzzed like an angry wasps' nest, I left for a long-arranged two-week course in Cheshire where I'd be revisiting the hired assassin Sparafucile. Those who remained kept me informed about the inquisition now taking place in East Sussex: I was glad to leave with my idyllic view of the place still intact.

My second attempt at Sparafucile revealed the extent of my progress. After almost four years with Paddy I finally had the freedom simply to open my voice and let rip, but, as at all new stages, I had a tendency to play with it constantly, to explore and stretch its limits. As with all singers 'the voice' seemed to be a separate entity with an independent existence. It was a naughty child I could disown when it didn't perform well. Yet for it to communicate successfully it had to be integral to me, my medium for expressing feelings and emotions which often found no other outlet. My plan had always been to acquire a technique, free my instrument, then forget about it so that it could express simply the different moods of the roles I had to portray, but now I felt as if I hadn't mastered it at all. It had possessed me. It wouldn't allow me to return to the singer I had been before I began training seriously, naked and exposed before an audience, when the sound was embryonic and flawed. I agonised over this, but couldn't deny that the sheer sensation of producing a big free sound was in itself extremely satisfying.

* * *

Before the start of my final year at college I took a couple of weeks off and went to London, where most of my Oxford friends now lived. My sister, Liz, who now lived and worked in Rome, would be there too. But it wasn't the reunion I'd anticipated. Passing the bathroom on the way to my old bedroom I heard repeated short breaths that might equally have been sobs or laughter. I knocked on the door and heard the bolt clack open with a sound resonant with childhood memories. Liz's eyes were red and tears rolled down her face.

'Dad's having an affair.'

'Who's doing the catering?'

I was genuinely relieved it wasn't something more serious.

'It isn't funny.'

'So how do you know?'

'His tracksuit bottoms. I knocked them over going upstairs. A packet of condoms fell out,' she sniffed.

'That doesn't prove a thing.'

'Mark.' She looked at me as if I too were trying to deceive her. 'He's such a bastard.'

'And?'

'I know. He'll never change. Poor Mum.'

'Mum's fine.'

'Mark, how can you say that? It's been unbearable for her.'

A few days later I was standing under a bus shelter on Finchley Road during the rush hour, trying to gain some protection from the pouring rain, when I noticed a woman with short black hair and heavy mascara, umbrella in one hand and in the other — I could scarcely believe it — a copy of one of Dad's novels. I'd never seen anyone reading his books in public before. It made me proud. But just as I prepared to step forward to tell her who I was she glanced at me, and I instinctively realised it was the wrong thing to do.

The book she was reading, *The Comic*, was one that had been out of print for years and happened, coincidentally, to be my favourite of his novels, perhaps because in the portrayal of its protagonist he'd come as close as he ever would to describing himself. Maybe he knew that, and that's why he'd given it to her, as I knew he had. This was her. Liz was right. I had no proof, I simply knew. On closer examination I noticed she was only at the start of the book. Perhaps it was only the beginning of the affair. She seemed tense and unhappy. I wondered who she was and how he'd met her.

Then, on the way home, I had the sort of insight years of therapy had never granted: Mum, in her anguish, had confided in me about Dad's womanising long before I was able to grasp its true significance and although, of course, I recognised her pain, I was at an age when I wanted to emulate Dad. In making me a confidant, Mum had also unwittingly set me up as his rival. In competing with Dad both as a womaniser and as a surrogate 'husband', somehow all seduction became tainted in my mind, unconsciously, with the stigma of incest. I'd never felt comfortable about seduction, preferring to wait for women to make the move, always expecting to be rebuffed. It had never felt right or healthy, and at last I felt I knew why.

Once home I jotted down my thoughts and hid them away like precious stones, never hinting at the fact I owned them. Although in a sense 'The Solution', as I called it, might be construed as an abnegation of responsibility, I actually ended up feeling closer to both my parents. What followed was a wonderful sense of release from guilt, and greater self-liking. Ironically I started to have affair after affair, sometimes keeping two or three in the air at the same time, mastering the art of juggling that had always eluded me. The genie of my libido had finally been released and Pentheus destroyed. It wasn't so much that I was emulating Dad as enjoying a liberation, much the same way as I was revelling in my newfound vocal freedom.

* * *

As the blinds went up and light poured through the windows, illuminating some of the darker corners of my own life, Mark Raphael, my first singing teacher, was nearing the end of his.

I went to see him in hospital where he lay, half-asleep. At last the extended Indian summer, that had blessed him ever since I'd first known him, was coming to an end. After the throat cancer, a stroke had paralysed him down one side of his neck, but he'd never stopped singing. At the age of eighty he'd made me tapes of the lieder, chansons and English song that had formed his core repertoire, including some delightful ones he had written himself. Worn though his voice was, there was no barrier between it and the source of his expression, so it still moved me more than most voices. After I'd seen him I played his tapes again. They reminded me of other rooms in my life where the lights had gone out, of how far I'd strayed from simple communication in my obsession to achieve sound. Mark had been very distressed when I told him they were training me as a bass. He felt it was wrong, and though the offers I was receiving wouldn't, on the surface, justify his fears, the fact that I still felt so alien to the stock characters of that voice's repertoire perhaps did.

His memorial service was held at the Reform synagogue in Marble Arch for which, I only learned now, he'd written a great deal of music. Despite Dad's daily reminders of our provenance, albeit accompanied with caveats that we weren't thoroughbreds, I'd never actually been inside a synagogue before. None of us had been blessed, bar or bat-mitzvahed, the ritual of Shabbat was going to football matches, Easter was celebrated rather than Pesach, Christmas as opposed to Channukah. Lapsed? As Woody Allen once said, 'My Rabbi's so Reform he's a Nazi.' So I went with very mixed feelings, excited at the prospect of entering a shul for the first time, even if the occasion was a sad one. I certainly nurtured no expectation of returning to the fold. Years of Oxford philosophy had drummed out any vestigial religious belief. Passing through the hall my arm was tugged and someone proffered me a scruffy black paper kippa. I was so beyond redemption even this custom was unknown to me, but then, as I walked into the temple itself, I experienced a wonderful inner tranquillity. It was something I'd never encountered in countless churches and chapels where, if anything, I was always edgy. I felt an almost physical sensation of belonging.

The choir sang Mark's music and I remembered how it had begun for him. In an East End stiebel they'd recognised his talent and paid for him to go and study voice in Milan, hoping he might find the fortune there to keep him out of the soup queue. I wanted to know more about Mark's Jewishness. When the Rabbi asked for silence, I closed my eyes and saw him as he'd been when we first met, impish and radiant. I started to cry. Everyone did. There weren't many Jews in the synagogue, Mark's world was a secular one. I wondered whether it was love for him that united us, gave us all, Jew and gentile alike, a sense of belonging there. I kissed the tattered paper kippa, folded it and put it in my pocket.

* * *

The next hat I wore was a crown. After trying me out in a couple of tiny roles, Opera North gave me my major debut, as the King of Clubs in their new production of Prokofiev's *Love for Three Oranges*. It was directed by Richard Jones and conducted by David Lloyd-Jones, both of whom I'd worked with at college. There was nothing regal about Opera North's Green Room with its battered old tables and chairs, peeling walls and nicotine-stained ceiling. A curious upstairs/downstairs system operated, principals on the higher level with the fag smoke, chorus on the lower.

Playing opposite me as my son the prince was Peter Jeffes, the only other student of Mark Raphael's still working in the profession. As was so often to be the case, despite playing the most senior role in the opera I was probably the most junior member of the cast. I watched from my vantage point, listening to the comments and assessments of the chorus while each soloist arrived for the first rehearsal. In strode a bronzed individual, dapper in white chinos and sports jacket. He smiled at everyone before risking a coffee.

'Oh how delightful, Peter Jeffes!' someone sneered.

'End of tea-break!' yelled the ASM.

Our first production meeting was in the company's brand new rehearsal room, accessible from the theatre via a covered bridge, a converted porn cinema restored to Edwardian neobaroque. Such luxury was almost pampering after the squalor on the other side. I introduced myself to Peter and revealed our connection. He seemed more shocked than pleased.

Richard Jones, the producer, stood by the mock-up of the set, chewing his eternal gum, neck thrust forward, shoulders back. 'Don't ever stand like this!' he'd once warned me. I greeted him and watched a smile cross his face like the sun between two clouds.

'How are you?' he asked unenthusiastically, then carried on chewing his gum, scrutinising the arriving cast as if we were already in production. When he was satisfied all were present he began, in a nasal, deadpan voice.

'I want to bring out some of the darker elements of this piece. It's a fairy story but it's also very weird and strange. Have a look at these pictures. They're from productions by Meyerhold. They'll give you an idea of the sort of physicality I want to achieve.'

I was to set the scene with a mimed sequence in which I collapsed to the ground in despair while a court herald explained that my son's hypochondria is the cause of my predicament. Although we went over it endlessly, I couldn't satisfy Richard. It wasn't smooth enough; there wasn't enough line through it; I didn't have sufficient control of my body. Matters didn't improve in the afternoon. Scene One was an extended aria for the King, and Richard wanted most of it sung from the throne. After the morning's efforts, that came as a relief. But then:

'Mark! You're not singing *The Messiah*! You've got to energise it much, much more! It needs the quality of despair. Does that make sense?' he chewed.

Each director I worked with became a surrogate for my sadistic nanny, and having my movement scrutinised still created an inner tension that blocked my natural instinct and led me into bad dramatic judgments. Richard took me aside later.

'Mark, I was watching you during the tea break and you look as if you've done Alexander, so what happens when you start performing?'

I was handed over to his assistant whose eccentric appearance and demeanour, as with practically everyone involved in the production, made him almost indistinguishable from the characters portrayed on stage. This was necessary but depressing, since, as far as I knew, I was the only one who had been singled out for extra coaching. My only consolation was that I'd been employed to do the role, so someone must have had faith in me. By the end of the third week and the first run through of Act One I thought I'd found a sufficiently bizarre walk for my character. But Richard caught me as I was leaving the rehearsal.

'Mark, make sure you don't get caught up in Leander's physicality. It isn't appropriate. Does that make sense?' and he nodded as if in agreement with himself.

In the course of the following week Richard and Tim were too concerned with managing all the big choral scenes to worry about me, so I started to explore and experiment, and as I did so I began to understand my character and his movement. My ponderous, stooped walk was beginning to engender the feelings of a man laden with the usual bass *Weltschmerz* I'd found in Arkel. The mime sequence that had caused me so much grief, in which I stretched my hands imploringly towards the sky, clenched them, brought them painfully into my chest, then collapsed to the ground, staring in despair towards the audience with a look of total horror on my face before thumping the floor with my fists in time to the brass chords, was now the lynchpin of my performance. The extreme gestures it required somehow engendered the correct feeling for the rest of the role. When Richard rewarded me with a deadpan 'Good, Mark,' it felt like beating the scousers at Anfield.

On the first night I drew a deep breath and headed to the wigs department for the uncomfortable, hour-long process of transformation. A plastic bald-cap was pulled tightly over my head, depriving it of all air and light for the next five hours. Then came the spirit gum, cold and cloying. Spidery lines were drawn from my eyes, out and over my cheekbones.

''Old the sides fer us can yer, ta!'

I could smell the gin on the wigs girl's breath.

'Good night last night?'

'Aye! Got really pissed!'

'Makes a change.'

'Ah know! Gettin' a bit mooch in't it?'

She grinned sheepishly. On went the heavy wig, its long strands of nicotine-coloured string dangling from the back of my head down to my shoulders. My moustache was absurdly long tonight, its wispy extensions descending almost to my chest. I couldn't wait to go.

''Ang on! Ah in't finished yet. Ah've got ter put yer eyebrows on.'

Out came a pair that made Denis Healey's look plucked. I could barely see.

I caught myself in the mirror, split between the neck and torso of a young man, and the face and hair of a nonagenarian troll – partly myself, partly what I'd become – and suddenly I was there, exposed before a packed theatre, taking my first stride forward.

'*The King of Clubs is in distress*,' sang the Herald as I raised my hands slowly upwards, straining to achieve a fluid line.

'*For his son . . .*'

I crashed to the floor on all fours without losing the flow, dropped my head, and felt a cold draught at the back of my neck. The wig had flipped over my face. It wasn't glued at the back. My only hope was that in such a crazy show people might assume it was deliberate. I raised my head and stared manically at the audience, thus jolting the wig back into place. No one seemed to notice. 'If all shows were as enjoyable as this,' wrote one critic, 'opera might get a good name.' Fortunately for me the managements in Lisbon, Tel Aviv, Edinburgh and Maastricht appeared to agree.

VARIATION FOUR

The Jew

VARIATION FOUR – *The Jew*

Ge-
Trunken hast du,
Was von den Vatern mir kam
Und von jenseits der Vater:
Pneuma

(You have drunk,
what came to me from my forefathers
and from beyond my forefathers:
Breath)

'Benedicta', Paul Celan

A month after opening, *For the Love of Three Oranges* arrived in Manchester where I would have to prove that my time at the Royal Northern hadn't been wasted. I stayed with Sara, an old college friend, whose landlady was herself an aspiring singer. Julia was descended from a line that had begun for me with Rossetti's Francesca da Rimini and continued, via Leonardo, through Louise the heroine of my schoolboy dreams. Her hair had the familiar length and tight, curling texture, not jet black like Louise's but dark honey, her vivacious blue eyes set off by a dark complexion, and her full lips and wide nose made me wonder whether, like Louise, she hadn't a West Indian grandmother. Although this was our first meeting, we had already spent hours on the phone when I'd called to speak to Sara, and we'd struck up a rapport without knowing what the other looked like.

I was convinced that my meeting with Julia was fated, that all that had gone before had merely been preparation for this latest incarnation of my perfect woman. And I was now no longer a tormented, tongue-tied adolescent but, rather like Prince Gremin whose aria I sang at my every concert and audition, weary of the shallow frivolity of so many recent relationships, and waiting for a Tatyana to illuminate my life 'like a star in jet black night'. Fortunately, Julia's classic singer's earthiness anchored my feelings and stopped me flying off heavenwards.

'You look a lot younger in the flesh than you do on stage. I thought I was going to have some dirty old man dribbling round my house. It must be hard to act someone ten years older than yourself!'

'More like seventy!'

Ten years. That had to be the age gap between us.

'You have to understand,' Sara explained, 'with Mutley, nothing she ever says is serious.'

'I beg your pardon. I'm very serious indeed.'

'Why Mutley?'

'Haven't you heard her laugh? She sounds just like him.'

Mutley, Dick Dastardly's cartoon canine assistant: I used to do impressions of his breathy, nasal snigger. The name Julia was serious, a Roman matron; Mutley softened her and endeared her to me even more.

'I thought you were someone else.'

'Who?'

'I asked Sara what you looked like, and she said "Well, 'e's tall, an' 'e's got dark 'air," and I thought you were that Liverpool bloke.'

'Roberto the Scouser. But he's got a full head of hair.'

'Well, you know Sara. She doesn't notice such things, bless her.'

'Pardon! I never said 'e looked like Roberto.'

'Well, there you go. At least I don't look like the King of Clubs.'

'Oh, I don't know. Same hair style,' replied Julia, going off into her Mutley laugh.

My determination to win Julia was fuelled by overwhelming need. I well knew what the Royal Northern was like and the chances of someone like her escaping its libidinous clutches, so, after the *Oranges* shows were over I found an excuse to return to Manchester, the city that until recently I'd been so keen to escape. Ostensibly I was coming to see Sara, but it was Julia who answered the door, voluptuous in a tight, black sweatshirt set off by an ankle-length, cream skirt. She sat next to me on the leather sofa where I'd spent the night on my previous visit fantasising about how things might have developed had I been sharing her bed.

Did she have any West Indian blood? I had to know how far her similarity to Louise extended. She exploded with laughter.

'Oh, I can't wait to tell my parents!'

'Well, you do look as if you might have.'

'How?'

'You're dark and your mouth . . .'

'Thanks a lot!'

'It's a compliment. I've always . . .'

'What?'

I was revealing my hand long before I'd intended to.

'Well, I think black girls are gorgeous.'

'Actually, half my relations are rabbis.'

* * *

Sara and Dave joined us for dinner at a local Nepalese restaurant. For some reason Dave ordered 'a small dry sherry' instead of his usual pint of lager, and I called him a pretentious twat, an off-the-cuff insult which elicited an unexpectedly gratifying response from Julia, as tears of laughter streamed down her face. Again I was hit by a sense of déjà vu, but this time it was deeper, as if it wasn't her type that I'd known before but herself, all along.

Later, upstairs in her bedroom we sat discussing modern art until the words became a backdrop to the language of our bodies and the undulating motion of the lake beneath her bed sucked us into its depths, Klimtesque figures mirroring the ones on her wall, entwined on the kaleidoscopic patterns of her bedspread. I didn't want to leave that painting. I would have been happy for posterity to accept its engraving of us at that moment, as joyful as Paolo and Francesca at the instant of their only kiss before Gianciotto's knife descended.

Time and place served only to add dimension and colour to the canvas. In the solipsism of its early state, every word of *The Tempest* seemed written with us in mind.

> . . . *Full many a lady*
> *I have eyed with best regard; and many a time*
> *The harmony of their tongues hath into bondage*
> *Brought my too diligent ear: for several virtues*
> *Have I liked several women; never any*

With so fun a soul, but some defect in her
Did quarrel with the noblest grace she owed
And put it to the foil: but you, o you,
So perfect and so peerless, are created
Of every creature's best.

Julia had fallen asleep on my shoulder by the time Ferdinand was confessing my love.

* * *

'Can she cook?'

I was thrilled by my godfather's reference to the banal practicalities of day-to-day life. It meant that at least he foresaw a future for us, in a real world that would continue to exist once the magic of the one we now inhabited might have faded – the very idea of cleaning and cooking together had immense appeal, the sealing of a bond rather than a chore.

'Why don't you two come over and stay with me in New York?'

The Royal Northern had come through with a large, unexpected scholarship that would enable me to pursue my study of singing with a teacher or in a country of my choice, so I chose New York, where, by a helpful concatenation of circumcisions, as Dad might have said, the mentor to three of the finest basses in the world resided. Julia, sadly, was in the middle of term, and I flew across the Atlantic, for this short period, alone.

Parallels and contrasts with my first solo trip to Italy struck me as I did so. Then, having travelled with the intention of studying singing, I discovered more about myself than my larynx, thanks to my relationship with the daughter of Dad's old friend. Now I was journeying with the same purpose and staying with another of his closest friends. Rather than going to university, Dad had spent those years convalescing from tuberculosis in Rome and Florence, where he met the men who were to prove his lifelong friends. My godfather, Stanley Moss, was one of them, David in Florence another. To me they represented aspects of a young Dad that hadn't developed but fossilized. I travelled all over the world to meet them, even though his present life was a constant place I could always visit. Yet, at the same time, I felt like the enchanted child escaping from the witch's house only to find that every path returned me there. Even three thousand miles away I saw his face and wondered why I'd journeyed so far to meet him.

My art-dealer/poet/publisher godfather lived in a mansion in Riverdale, the wealthy part of the Bronx. El Greco and Tiepolo rubbed noses, their saints and apostles gazing down on Horatio, Stanley's golden retriever, brushing his tail against a Zurbarán. Stanley was also an opera fanatic who'd seemingly heard most of the twentieth century's great singers, many of them whilst perched in an eyrie at the top of the Met, so he was happy to play host to my ambitions, and add obscene descants as I sang for my supper in the presence of other art dealers, poets and intellectuals. The expanse and extent of New York's Jewish population, through which one could move unimpeded by a gentile for miles, meant that Stanley had not been forced to assimilate culturally as Dad had, but although he and his friends were ostensibly more confident than their English counterparts, they were also more sensitive to anti-Semitism, latent and actual. Stanley's poetry, quintessentially Jewish, though not religious in an accepted sense, articulated many of my own more arcane feelings:

> *The man who never prays*
> *Accepts that the wheat field in summer*
> *Kneels in prayer when the wind blows across it,*
> *That the wordless rain and snow*
> *Protect the world from blasphemy.*
> *His wife covers him with a blanket*
> *On a cold night — it is, perhaps, a prayer?*
> (from 'The Blanket')

I started to examine the poetry of Paul Celan and Osip Mandelstam, whose books formed part of Stanley's own extensive poetic library, and in them I found a Jewish spirituality with which I could identify, even if in the process I became guilty of repeating my father's heresy of setting up an atheistic Trinity in place of the one, indivisible Lord of scripture. I also learned from one of Stanley's dinner guests that song was considered in the Kabbalah to be an even higher form than poetry, *intense being that disappears*, as opposed to a poem which, though it has the power to catch something that is about to disappear, coarsens, captures and clothes it.

A twenty minute walk followed by an hour-long, seventeen stop subway ride took me from Riverdale to my singing teacher on the Upper West Side, though after I'd witnessed two assaults, a crack addict handling live ammunition and a hood concealing a hand gun, my godfather thought it might be better if I took the stockbroker train to Grand Central.

'You're simply naht that big, booming singer you're presenting yourself as,' came the disheartening verdict, and soon Paddy's conceptual approach was replaced by a rigorous physical discipline. An insecure singer, I was delighted by the apparent security of the concrete technique on offer. Now, instead of aiming indiscriminately for somewhere in the head and tinting the vowels with a touch of 'ur' or 'aw', I was channeling the sound into a specific region above the lip, behind the nose, feeling it ascend and descend with the pitch I was singing, as if hitting the notes on a xylophone. Meanwhile a diaphragmatic support was being manoeuvred into position that would keep the sound in place at all times. It seemed to give my voice clarity and cutting edge, but it felt alien. More than ever I felt enslaved by technique, but whereas before I felt the end had been to release my natural voice, now it seemed that one was being imposed which might earn me money, but at the expense of my integrity. I might as well have had a tape recording of another singer up my nose. To confuse matters further, my new technique was achieving results. New York City Opera, Baltimore, Pittsburgh and Milwaukee all offered me work on the strength of auditions, so there seemed no ostensible reason to question my teaching. Quite the reverse. Yet I knew that, despite it all, I wasn't being truthful to the self I was at last beginning to understand. I would eventually pay a heavy price for that infidelity.

* * *

Back in England I was keen to show off my new sound but, like a cat with a freshly trapped bird, I was disappointed by my cool reception. It confirmed my instinct that, despite the enthusiastic response in the States, it wasn't right. 'I don't like it at all!' Mum confided in Julia. I decided that New York's number one singing teacher and the impresarios of four American opera companies probably knew better than me, and suppressed my natural impulses. Nor did I fear that my new approach might be called into question, since I had work extending as far as the horizon, and it didn't occur to me that the waters of the ocean beyond might submerge me.

> *Drowning simply wet him*
> *And sent the blood off*
> *In water like smoke*

wrote my godfather of Paul Celan's suicide. I became obsessed with Celan – the pain and guilt of a man who, alone of all his family, had survived the Holocaust and was forced to express himself in the language of their murderers because 'only in the mother tongue can one speak his own truth', the language in which so much of what I wanted or needed to read was written. But each time I began to study it, I bit through its shiny surface into something bitter and rotten, as if it, my own mother's tongue, were rejecting me.

> *Fahlstimmig, aus*
> *der Tiefe geschunden:*
> *kein Wort, kein Ding,*
> *und beider einziger Name*
>
> *fallgerecht in dir*
> *fluggerecht in dir*
>
> *wunder Gewinn*
> *einer Welt*
> (from Paul Celan's 'Lichtzwang' 2.307)

(Pale voice driven from the depths; not a word, not a thing, and of both the same name, fallen right in you, flown right in you, wondrous gain of a world)

Davar, the Hebrew for both 'word' and 'thing', was the language of the identity beneath the German poem. Crunching through the German of Celan, I tasted an entire cultural and linguistic legacy.

* * *

When *Oranges* was revived in the spring, I went to live with Julia, watering the seeds of our love. Its soil was fertile. Julia took a pregnancy test while I was performing in Leeds and broke the news to me over the phone. I struggled to shut out the sound of her weeping as I sat on the King of Clubs' throne, bewailing my son's ailments, closer than I'd ever felt before to the truth of paternal emotion. But this was for her, my Bagel as I called her, so much younger than me, still half a child herself, whom I wanted to hold and console, though before I could, Fata Morgana would have to fall on the floor and show her knickers, the audience would be scratching and sniffing while Farfarello farted, a giant rat would be drawn across the stage and I would pronounce the death sentence on an Addams family of villains.

It was too soon, yet at the same time so right, like a confirmation that our union had been destined. I held her that night in a way I'd never held anyone before, as a lover but without a lover's arousal, and as a father to her and all she was at that moment, partner, daughter, mother. I was ready for all those feelings I'd rejected with other lovers or

only ever played with before on stage or in rehearsal. Anxious
and upset as we were, this felt like the final union. I told her
that whatever she decided I would go with her. Neither of
us had the means, nor did our relationship seem established
enough to support a child, despite the instinct that touched
us both, which said that didn't matter, this was right.

We drove to a clinic in Stockport very early one morning, in
the Morris Maxi Julia had had sprayed bright pink, and sat in
the waiting room, surrounded by anxious girls even younger
than Julia, breakfast television's insensitive clang silencing
unspeakable thoughts. 'We're *wide* awake!' It didn't need
the constant repetition.

'Only a hoover, it sucks it out of the womb': the mundane
image was chastening if inaccurate. Northern pragmatism —
that's what was needed at this time, none of that arty-farty
navel-searching and its accompanying self-pitying wallow.
   Julia limped as she came towards me and burst into tears
on my shoulder. I hadn't been able to stop thinking of her
lying on a table, being poked and searched, helpless, a child,
giving herself to be . . . what? There was nothing to cure.
This was choice, self-imposed. We'd passed the anti-abortion
protesters in the car. But my Bagel was hurt, and if anyone
I was to blame. It was my irresponsibility too. Yet our pain,
our experience, our feelings were uniting us, forming us into
a couple, with the blood-bond of battle-hardened comrades.

In the days that followed she bled profusely and I didn't want
to leave her for a second. The operation was botched and
she had to go in again before serious infection took hold. I
wanted to bump into those anti-abortion demonstrators now,

break apart their placards and kick fuck out of them. Why did they think people came here? It hadn't been easy for many, young kids who couldn't cope and might be wounded for life. They needed to be loved and pitied, cared for in the way they might have wanted to love and care for the children they felt unable to bring into the world. 'They're right, Mark. I've done a terrible thing.' Julia was safe now, but our mourning was just beginning, for the baby who was never to be. I wondered whether fate had meant that too.

Several weeks later I came home to find an apricot toy poodle puppy called, suitably androgynously, Cherubino bounding about the living room. I wasn't pleased.

'You realise this means we're tied,' I prophesied. 'We won't be able to go on holiday. It'll have to come with us everywhere, it'll need constant feeding and attention, and you can clean up the mess!'

But it wasn't long before I recommended the purchase of Cherubino's mate.

* * *

May it be thy will, o Lord our God, and God of our fathers, that we walk in thy Law and hold fast to thy commandments. The translated parts I could understand of the synagogue services I began attending to discover more about my newfound culture, meant far less to me than the guttural, aspirated sections I didn't, evoked by curves, dashes, squares and dots, abstract pictures transcending the totality of the words themselves, coupling, dancing and swimming across the page, angels that lived in my prayer book.

We are the music makers
And we are the dreamers of dreams

Rabbi Friedlander frequently informed us, quoting O'Shaughnessy. The London synagogue where Julia's brother had been married was happy to accept another member of his family without asking too many questions, though it didn't hurt that Dad was a well-known English Jew. In fact the organ-accompanied Reform service's German roots were much more closely entwined with Mum's than Dad's, though thanks to the organist, who like Mark Raphael had been brought up in the East End, most of the musical settings were orthodox in content and spirit, and it was to this element that I responded. I was transported by their soulful pathos, whose roots stretched far beneath the floor of the grand, genteel Victorian room in which the services were held.

One regular member of the synagogue's congregation fascinated me, the shammas (senior warden) who sat by the side of the ark in top hat and morning suit, leading the prayers in fluent Hebrew, holding aloft the Torah scroll, guiding congregants in coping with the *mitzvoth* (blessings) bestowed during services. Whereas others seemed to be going through a routine, he was inspired by genuine religious fervour. I watched in admiration as he took three steps forward then three back before the recitation of the Eighteen Blessings, bent his knees as he uttered the word *Baruch* (Bless), bowed as he said *Atah* (You), then straightened, immersed in a ritual that I imagined was close to the kabbalistic *devekut* (cleaving to God) I'd read about.

Before long I'd taught myself enough Hebrew to follow most

of the prayers and was familiar enough with the music to be able to sing them. Gradually the rest of the congregation stopped singing and listened. I was concentrating too hard on the Hebrew text to worry about what noise I was making, but the plaintive music resonated with me in much the same way as Celan's poetry and the jokes I'd learned from Dad, and I wasn't performing but rather interpreting and expressing it through the medium of myself and giving it, in its purest, most cathartic form, back to the congregation. Any joy or relief they experienced was a delight to me, gratifying because I had helped them in some way, given them whatever it was they came to synagogue for. Not since my concerts at Oxford, when uncluttered emotional intent had been sabotaged by faulty technique, had I felt so fulfilled by singing and its effect.

'*Hashem* has given you a great gift,' the devout shammas informed me one morning. Tears came to my eyes on finally receiving the acceptance I'd so long looked for without, until now, ever really knowing from whom it was I'd sought it.

After synagogue I'd often go to a match. The services finished, conveniently, before one, although I was assured this wasn't because the Rabbi was a QPR supporter. On my way to Stamford Bridge one afternoon I noticed a burly bloke in a T-shirt sporting the challenge 'Chelsea FC Pride of London', striding down the middle of the road as if prepared to take on all comers. I found it hard to reconcile him with the zealous shammas. Enlightenment came the following week, after he'd led the *kiddush* blessings over wine and bread.

'Oh yeah! That was me. There's a lot of Chelsea in this shul. The Chairman's one. He's got a season ticket.'

I later found out over a cup of coffee in Debenhams department store, where we'd gone to check out the women's lingerie he sold for a living, that he was as passionate about black music as he was about football and Judaism. He was my doppelgänger. We'd been born at the same time, grown to the same height, and had the same colouring and follicular deficiency, but it was the single-minded passion with which we pursued our shared interests that most united us. Stephen's ecstatic displays irritated certain members of the congregation who'd joined a Reform synagogue to escape such things, but they lent the services a spiritual quality that elevated them above mere ritual and routine. Conversely, the music I sang worked on a level of communication above the recitation of prayer. For me its ancient plaintiveness cut like a laser through centuries of history to establish a sense of spiritual continuity. 'Lord of the world', said a great Hassidic master, 'if I knew how to sing I wouldn't allow you to hide yourself up there in the infinite universe. I'd pursue you with my song and force you to descend among men.'

Yet for me it was never a question of believing in the God of the Torah, something precluded by a lifetime of sceptical rationalism, but the discovery of a spirituality which, whilst mine, was shared by everyone who responded to the service as I did. Chances were that those who shared that response would also share an outlook caught in the *pneuma*, the breath of Celan's sense of Jewishness, an essence, like music, that couldn't be caught, and codified in law or defined by race. I wasn't a racial or a religious Jew. I was a pneumatic Jew.

ARIA DA CAPO — THE VEDL

הרי את מקדשת לי בטבעת זו כדם משה וישראל

Behold thou art consecrated unto me, by this ring, according to the law of Moses and of Israel.

'We're going to a wedding, a lovely, lovely wedding.
We're going to a wedding in the Strand.
There'll be Mendelbaum and Finkelstein
And Apfelbaum and Silverstein.
We're going to a wedding in the Strand!'

Ours, in Knightsbridge, was a couple of miles to the west of the one in Dad's little song, but it was a proper Jewish one, held in synagogue under a chupah before the ark containing the Torah, conducted by a real rabbi, and with a lavish reception afterwards at Pinewood Studios.

Julia, who'd been raised in the community Dad had left behind on being sent to public school, never shared my passion for something that to her was merely a way of life and not some 'golden key to self', though she was happy to follow suit with the other members of her family and marry in synagogue. 'Only a goy would . . .' prefaced her frequent rebukes for the ignorance of a *Baal Teshuva* (born again Jew). The cultural crash-course I'd given myself, with the help of

249

my friend Stephen the shammas, would never set me on an equal footing with those who'd been raised in families where Jewish culture and tradition was the unquestioned backdrop. Although I knew, for example, that my *siddur* (prayer book) should always rest back to front in acknowledgement of the fact that Hebrew is read from right to left, I was still caught out saying 'I wish you long life', an accepted funeral formula, to an unmarried *mespocha* (relation) at a wedding, when what I meant to say was 'please God by you.' (Had I used the latter phrase at a funeral I might have faced permanent expulsion from my new club.) Even during the wedding ceremony I only narrowly avoided disaster, in my haste to be seen as fluent in Hebrew before I could read its alphabet properly, almost confusing a daleth, d, for a resh, r, and marrying my bride 'according to the pity' rather than the 'law' of Moses and Israel.

Julia had themed the wedding around our toy poodles, furry, apricot versions of the baby we hadn't had. Their kissing, sculpted likenesses even adorned the traditional tiered wedding cake, and the orange dresses and waistcoats of the bridesmaids, pageboys and attendants screamed their absence – the Rabbi had vetoed Julia's plan for them to trip down the aisle behind the bridal party dressed as canine versions of Mrs Shilling. Even Dad, relaxed and amenable, clearly a beneficiary (even if unwitting) of Mum's newly discovered healing powers, wore a waistcoat in their honour. Invisible trumpets pumped out the triumphal march from *Aida* to mark Julia's entrance, but the doors at the end of the aisle at first failed to open. When they did finally part, Julia emerged crying – yet serene, her eyes both giving and asking for love as we met beneath the chupah, and for a split second I had an uncanny vision of the many,

many times this had happened before, the final frames on the reel rushing through the projector, and, overcome with a sense of the power and fate of our love, I began to cry too. The song I'd chosen about Jerusalem, a yearning, cantorial cry for redemption. 'May it ever be a city of peace', rang out in that eternally vain wish. But it was good to wish; at times one caught glimpses of paradise, like rays of light through a stained glass window, in love and in music, as now. *'Mazel Tov!'* The glass cracked and splintered beneath my foot, the vision with it, and we were back in the reality of boisterous celebration.

'Who took the glass out of the plastic bag?' muttered the Rabbi, observing the myriad shards kaleidoscoping the carpet. This time it wasn't a Jewish ritual that my brother Toby, in his guise as best man, had broken, but a more tangible local custom, with immediate, irritating consequences. I often wondered whether the Rabbi knew the truth about me. Each time I went for a pee in synagogue, I retracted my foreskin so as to appear circumcised. 'Does your father still go to West London synagogue?' he'd asked me a couple of times, seemingly party to information unavailable to me. It would have been nice to believe that Dad had been making secret trysts with the *Shechinah*, the female godhead, rather than whoever was the latest to inherit the umbrella of the sad creature at the Finchley Road bus stop. At the Sabbath service the day before the wedding he behaved as I imagined he always had at synagogue, chatting and joking through the service, heedless of the angry, headmistressy looks he was receiving from the chairman's wife sitting directly behind him. Yet, unmindful as he was of the Jewish rituals I longed to enjoy and understand, he could just sit there like a naughty schoolboy, fart and belch if he fancied, and simply be the thing I wanted to be but, in spite of everything, wasn't.

Julia and I entered our reception, held in the vast ballroom of the Georgian mansion at Pinewood Studios where much of *The Great Gatsby* had been shot, to a small-scale version of the roar that greets the teams leaving the players' tunnel at Wembley. There were lads I'd stood beside on the United Road, singers who bellowed duets with me from the operatic stage, academics who'd studied with me at Oxford, Jews who prayed with me in synagogue, all of them aspects of who I was, all people I cared for, and who cared for me, us, and for a moment I understood that I had no need to try to be any one of those personae. I was none of them wholly, all of them partly, ultimately myself and accepted as such; or not. 'I only want people there who wish us well,' Julia had said.

The speeches, an all-male affair, three from the Glanville family and one from Julia's dad, reminded me of a meal I'd once served with four different types of meat and no vegetables. Overloaded with the badges, banners, shirts and scarves of Judaism, I inflected my own address with Yiddish cadences much as I'd once adopted the lazy twang of the Cockney Reds who seemed to have been the inspiration for my brother's speech, 'What can I say about Mark that the judge hasn't already in his summing up at the court case? . . . After I was born he became the first two-year-old to be treated for post-natal depression . . . I wish I'd met Julia before Mark, because then I could have warned her. His bedroom was like a shrine to Manchester United. It made the Sistine Chapel look like a pagan afterthought.'

'I can't follow that!' Dad lied, rising to deliver an uncus-
tomary groom's father's address, a version of his nightly
stand-up routine, seeking acceptance from his audience with
jokes about acceptance, tangible, or at least audible tokens
that he was loved, sending people diving for cover under a
hail of friendly fire. 'I told this joke to the Rabbi yesterday
and got no response, but if he laughs this time I'll know
I'm in. I'll give up writing and become a stand-up comic!
So there's this American Jew . . .' and then, as so often
before, Mum's hearty whoop came in like an exclamation
mark, emphasising to all present that her husband was about
to tell a joke, and that even if they didn't laugh, she would,
and I was reminded of how much, in spite of everything, she
still loved and supported him. '. . . and he's standing outside
this synagogue in Peking on Shabbas, and the Chinese Rabbi
comes up to him and says, "Are you Jewish?"

'"Well, sure!" answers the American.

'"You don' rook Jewish!"'

As the day progressed my gentile features began to show
through the Jewish mask. When Julia and I were hoisted
aloft on chairs to the accompaniment of the *Hora*, I waved
the handkerchief I'd been thrown at our encircling friends
instead of sharing it with my bride as a symbol of our new
bond. And I joined in with the singing of *Mazel Tov* as I cut
the cake when I should have been smilingly acknowledging
the blessing of our family and friends. I wasn't alone in my
ignorance. Hardly anyone seemed to know the tune, let alone
the words of the Israeli national anthem *Ha Tikvah* (Hope), a
failing which was thrown into relief by a passionate rendition
of the Welsh anthem, courtesy of my mother-in-law and her
relations. Even my seriously Jewish brother-in-law asked us

to raise our glasses to recently elected Yitzhak Rabin, 'the new president of Israel', when he should have been toasting old-established Chaim Herzog. Yet the proofs and gestures of membership, like the discarded programmes and scarves after a United defeat, were swept away by the spirit of the occasion. As the band played on, I felt like Tony in *West Side Story* facing Maria for the first time when everything and everyone else in the room starts to hum and blur like a spinning top.

I looked into my new bride's tear-stained eyes and saw them open like Venus fly-traps.

'I could kill your brother!'

'Why?'

'That frock coat he put you in. It's ten times too big.'

It hadn't occurred to me.

'Notice how beautifully his own fits.'

'Nu?' I shrugged my shoulders, like the stock hero of a thousand Jewish jokes. Rather like Abey in the menswear shop, I'd long since given up hope of finding a suit that actually fitted.

The author and publisher of this work are grateful to the proprietors listed below:

to Chatto & Windus both for permission to quote from *Remembrance of Things Past* by Marcel Proust, in Scott Moncrieff and Terence Kilmartin's translation, and from *On Identity* by Admin Maalouf in Barbara Bray's translation; to Methuen for permission to quote from *The Woman* by Edward Bond; to Suhrkamp Verlag for permission to quote from *Gesammelte Werke* by Paul Celan; and to Anvil Press for permission to quote from 'Asleep in the Garden' by Stanley Moss

We have made every reasonable effort to trace all copyright holders of quoted material, apologise for any omissions and are happy to receive emendations from copyright holders.